The Time Was...

"When Life was Simple...
   Faith and Friendship Strong."

Claudette Hood Howell

To: Sue Cook
With all good wishes and hope
that memories and your own
family history will come alive
for you and your children!

Claudette Hood Howell
June, 1997

Copyright © 1987
by **Claudette Hood Howell**
435 Hickory Hills Drive
Stone Mountain, GA 30083

All Rights Reserved. No part of this book may be reproduced in any form or by any means without the prior written permission of the author, excepting brief quotes used in connection with reviews, written specifically for inclusion in a magazine or newspaper.

Cover design by **John Kollock**

Library of Congress Catalog Card Number 87-51388
ISBN: 0-9619794-0-2
2nd Printing May, 1988
1st Printing October, 1987

Printed in the United States of America

SOUTHEASTERN PUBLISHING CORPORATION
195 Newton Bridge Road
Athens, GA 30607

Dedication

This book is dedicated with love and gratitude to my parents, the Reverend and Mrs. Claude E. Hood, of Cleveland, Georgia, as a tribute to them for the love they have shown and the values and beliefs they have taught...

...to the memory of my grandparents and other relatives for the rich heritage they have left...

...to my children, in the hope they will benefit from the legacy that is theirs; that knowing of their heritage may help them in building their future...

...and to all others, who have roots in the hills of northeast Georgia, that they may find pleasant memories of yesteryear in remembering...THE TIME WAS...WHEN LIFE WAS SIMPLE...FAITH AND FRIENDSHIP STRONG.

Contents

Introduction vii

PART I

Home Of The Cherokees 1

Georgia And Her Counties 5

Life Was Simpler 15

Farming Was A Way Of Life 35

Reading, Writing, And Ciphering 53

Homemade Remedies 59

Yesterday's Words And Phrases 65

Cooking Was A Tradition 69

PART II

Baptist And Methodist Influences 77

The Early Years 89

The Ministerial Years 111

Funeral Customs 135

The Center Of Each Community 147

Camp Meetings 203

Photograph Album 205

Bibliography 211

Introduction

The cover of this book was beautifully painted by North Georgia artist, John Kollock. It is a composite of the people and the places that were important in the life of my dad, Reverend Claude Edward Hood.

The front cover depicts him baptizing in a river, the original Mt. View Baptist Church building, and his father's farm in White County, where Dad spent his growing-up years. The back cover is taken from photographs of my grandfather Wiley Hood, on his mule, Dad in the field plowing, the homeplace on Mossy Creek where I grew up, in White County, with Mother standing on the porch and me in the yard, and finally the ornate little church that graces the peaceful Nacoochee Valley, Crescent Hill Baptist Church, where Dad pastored during the 1940's.

This book has been written for many reasons, but primarily, it is to pay special tribute to my father for his many years of love and dedicated service to God and his fellowman. It is also a brief glimpse into the life of this minister, his family, members of his congregations, and others who composed the small, rural communities that were tucked into the hills and valleys of northeast Georgia, each one centered around the church.

While growing up as a minister's daughter, I was fortunate enough to meet people and make friends whom I would have otherwise never known. As I watched the years swiftly moving by and began having to give up many of those friends to disease, or just age itself, I realized that I could only remember parts of stories which they had told, and dates and events of our friendships were becoming less clear. There were more and more questions for which I wanted answers, and although those who were gone could no longer give me the answers themselves, there were people still here who could. My resolve to permanently record and document some of their stories became stronger when Dad retired as a pastor in 1984. Although he is still active today, Dad's earlier years could hardly be comprehended by our generation. Transportation in rural Georgia at that time was by horse, wagon, or on foot.

I felt that the lifestyles, good times, and friendships of people in the five northeast Georgia counties he pastored, over a period of fifty-five years, should be recorded for future generations. To record some of the good times, the warm memories, and various "how-to's," I have interviewed scores of folks and researched books, documents and records. Using this information, I have compiled in pictures and words a way for the reader to journey through a past life in northeast Georgia. The book begins with the days of the Cherokee Indians, highlights the lives of the early settlers, moves forward through wars, the Depression, and then into our modern-day world.

Throughout the book I have used a combination of pictures and references of my family, since these were readily available, as well as materials taken from other sources. My intent has been to use them to show and tell of a way of life that was common to most families in the area during the early years of Dad's ministry. Every effort has been made to assure accuracy in dates, events, and names; however, I found that there were often discrepancies resulting from handwritten records, word of mouth accounts, and recordings that were made a considerable time after the fact. Also, customs and traditions sometimes varied from one community to another.

This book is not intended to be used as a historical document, but rather as a vehicle by which you can begin your own journey into the history of the area and to better know the people of northeast Georgia. Herein you can see generations of families, places and lifestyles as all are changed by our movements through time.

If names, dates, or events recorded in this book are found to be in disagreement with your information, or if errors have been made, these were certainly not intentional. It is the spirit of the book and the joy of another time that I hope you will enjoy as you turn the pages.

I would like to thank all those people listed in the bibliography who assisted me in gathering information, and especially Mother and Dad, who patiently answered the hundreds of questions I have asked and who dug through dusty boxes and old records. My thanks to Dr. Frank Whittington, of Georgia State University, and to my friend Helene Mewborn, for having spent many hours editing copy, advising, and supporting me during the year it has taken to get this book ready for print. A very special thank you for the encouragement given me by my husband, Robert, without whom this book would not have been possible and to my children for their interest and support.

Lastly, I am grateful to those special people of northeast Georgia who have befriended me, from the time I first remember them when I was a very young girl, and who have remained my friends throughout these many years. I will always hold many fond memories of them all.

Claudette Hood Howell

Home Of The Cherokees

Those of our ancestors who came to the mountains of North Georgia in the late 18th and 19th centuries were brave souls. When they arrived, they found inhabitants living in the region who had for centuries called the mountains "home." Life was hard for these early pioneers, and only the strong survived. The weak fell by the wayside or they returned from whence they came.

When Spanish explorer Hernando de Soto led his European expedition through North Georgia in 1540, he found Indians living in the region. It is known that different tribes had lived in the region for centuries. While there is no exact record of when the Cherokee moved into the area, a large portion of North Georgia remained a part of the Cherokee Nation until 1838, when the Indians were forcibly removed from Georgia.

Legend says the beautiful Indian princess named Nacoochee, meaning "Evening Star," fell in love with a young brave named Sautee, of the hostile Choctaw tribe. The two lovers eloped, and the maiden's father organized a search party to find them. They were found on the slope of Mount Yonah, where Nacoochee's father commanded his braves to throw Sautee over the precipice. No sooner had the command been executed than Nacoochee flung herself after her lover. They were buried in one grave, and a mound was raised over them to mark the spot. The mound stands today in the middle of the Nacoochee Valley, located between Cleveland and Helen, Georgia. Another valley nearby bears the name of Sautee.

The ornate summerhouse peers from the undergrowth atop the Indian Mound in Nacoochee Valley. According to legend, the mound is the burial place of the Indian Princess Nacoochee, and her lover Sautee.

According to some historians, the legends of the Cherokees hold no actual truth. They are, in fact, only stories told repeatedly by the settlers about the Indians after their departure from the area. Whether story or truth, the telling offers the listener a romantic tale of bravery and the life that might have been lived by the earliest inhabitants of the virgin forests, valleys, and coves of the North Georgia mountains.

It is known that the Cherokees were not mound builders. They came into the area as the owners of the land after the Indians who were mound builders had been run out or had left on their own accord. The Cherokees are thought to be part of the Iroquois Nation, having moved from the north and settled throughout the southern mountain regions. Those who lived in Georgia were called the Lower Cherokees. Although the Cherokees were a peaceful people, they could be fierce warriors when necessary, and they were usually in a state of warfare with the Creek Indians, their neighbors to the south.

The Cherokee people were basically farmers, so they located most of their villages near rivers or other sources of fresh water. The rivers not only provided the supply of water they needed but also good bottom land for growing their crops. Occasionally, the river would overflow its banks and cause flooding in the villages. Interestingly, the Indian tribes had a flood legend similar to the Biblical story of Noah's flood.

Their crops consisted of corn, cotton, wheat, indigo, sweet and Irish potatoes, and tobacco. Apple and peach orchards were quite common as well as gardens filled with beautiful flowers of many hues. They hunted and fished to provide meat for their diets and also owned cattle and horses. Clay found in the riverbanks was used to make pottery and to plaster their houses and stockades. The Christian religion was embraced by many Cherokees, due primarily to the efforts of missionaries. The most numerous of the sects were the Moravians, Baptists, Methodists, and Prebyterians. Plants were respected by the Indians because many of them contained healing powers to help cure diseases.

It has been estimated that when the white man first penetrated the wilderness, perhaps 25,000 Cherokees were living in the area from North Georgia into the highlands of Kentucky. Over the next three centuries their realm was to be reduced by treaty after treaty until finally it was eradicated altogether.

When American independence was declared, several states had large bodies of western land, and Georgia was one of these states. Georgia's land extended as far west as the Mississippi River. In 1802, Georgia ceded the lands west of the state's present western boundary, to the United States, upon the condition that the government would remove the Indians from Georgia and do away with all titles and claims they might possess. Records indicated a population of about 11,000 Cherokees across the Cherokee Nation during the period before the advancing whites began to push them toward the Mississippi River. Through a series of treaties the Cherokees had left Habersham and Hall Counties, but they still held land west of the Chestatee River. The Cherokees and Creeks had longer and closer contact with the white man's civilization than any other group of Indians during the colonial and independence periods.

As lands were ceded by the Indians to the government, Georgia was opening up the state through land lotteries. These began in 1805, and continued through 1832. There were six lotteries in all conducted at Milledgeville, then the state capitol. The first major influx of white men to northeast Georgia came in 1819, as a result of the Cherokee Cessions of July 8, 1817 and February 27, 1819. The Legislative Acts were dated December 15, 1818. The county lines of Habersham were established about this time, having boundaries of 713 square miles. It then included what is now parts of White, Lumpkin, Rabun, and Stephens counties.

A census of the Cherokee Nation taken in November of 1825, showed the total number of Cherokees as being 13,783, with 1,277 Negro slaves being held in bondage. The following were listed as possessions of the Cherokees: black cattle, 22,531; horses, 7,683; hogs, 46,732; sheep, 2,566; goats, 330; looms, 762; spinning wheels, 2,486; wagons, 172; plows, 2,943; sawmills, 10; grist mills, 13; power mills, 1; blacksmith shops, 62; cotton gins, 8; schools, 18; turnpikes, 9; ferries, 18; and public roads, 20. This information was collected by official census takers of the United States and was not based merely on the opinions of the Cherokees or of their special friends. It showed the Cherokees were as well off as many of the white frontier people of the period.

In an effort to keep their land in Georgia and remain a self-governing nation, the Cherokees met on June 26, 1827, at New Echota (the capital of the Cherokee Nation) in west Georgia for the purpose of drafting a constitution for their nation. John Ross was president of the convention, which consisted of twenty-one delegates. All but nine who attended could write, and all but three had Christian names and surnames. The constitution which they adopted was patterned after that of the United States.

The Cherokees began the printing of their own newspaper the "Cherokee Phoenix," in 1828 at New Echota. It was the official organ of the Cherokee Nation and was published for six years, from 1828 until 1834, when it was suppressed by the Georgia authorities. Elias Boudinot, a full-blooded Indian, was the editor. Boudinot was educated in a Moravian school in New England, and after being adopted by Connecticut Congressman Elia Boudinot, was given his name. When Boudinot completed his education he returned to the Cherokee Nation.

Earlier, in 1821, the invention of a Cherokee alphabet made it possible for the "Phoenix" to be written and printed in the Cherokee language. Joe Guest (Sequoyah), who was a leader of the Cherokees, developed a syllabic form of writing which contained 86 characters, as compared to the white man's alphabet of 26 characters. Most Cherokees learned to read their new printed language in a short period of time.

The white man had wanted the Indians removed from Georgia since the early 1800's so they could claim the land for themselves. But it was the discovery of gold that brought about a renewed determination on the part of Georgia's governmental officials to take the land from the Cherokees at any cost. It is recorded that gold was first discovered on Duke's Creek in Habersham County, while others point to Ward's Creek in Indian Territory as being the first discovery. Ward's Creek was a western branch of the Chestatee River near present-day Dahlonega in what would later become Lumpkin County. Which discovery was first is of little consequence today as it relates to the effect it had on the Cherokee Nation. The gold, which the Indians had not disturbed for centuries, now brought about the ruin of their society and the end of the vast Cherokee empire in the East.

Toward the end of 1828, Georgia lawmakers passed legislation annexing the remaining Indian lands in northwest Georgia, and removing the rights of Cherokee citizens. The former Indian lands west of the Chattahoochee-Chestatee Rivers were mapped-out into counties and surveyed into land lots of 160 acres each and gold lots of 40 acres each. Distribution was by land lottery, with the holders of the lucky numbers winning the lots from the drawings. Married men could draw two numbers; single men and widows, one apiece. Indians were excluded and deprived of all legal protection and friendly counsel. With no land they could call their own, and no rights whatsoever under the white man's laws, the eastern Cherokees were literally a people without a land!

Over the next five years, the Cherokees were split into two factions: one group in favor of moving out of Georgia and the other against the move. John Ross, who was only one-eighth Indian, became the chief of the Cherokee Nation in 1828. He lived in a fine house at the head of the Coosa River where he combined the roles of merchant, planter, and statesman. He headed the group opposed to removal. "Cherokee Phoenix" editor Boudinot led the party supporting the move from Georgia. However, both groups knew it made little difference as to what they wanted. In the end, they would be forced to leave their home. In 1835, the Cherokee Nation signed the Treaty of New Echota, ceding to the United States all the remaining Indian territory east of the Mississippi River and giving up all rights to their Georgia land. A sum of $5 million, the promise of western lands (near present-day Tahlequah, Oklahoma), financing of the removal of the Indians, and one year's subsistence upon their arrival in Indian territory constituted the terms of the Treaty.

There are mixed reports as to the total number of Cherokees to be moved. The numbers vary from 17,000 (with 8,946 in Georgia) to 11,000 as recorded in different historical accounts. The government, convinced force was the only way the Cherokees could be removed from their lands, sent General Winfield Scott and 7,000 troups to enforce the eviction. The Indians were rounded-up and placed into stockades. Several hundred Indians managed to escape into the hills and hide from the white soldiers. From this remnant evolved today's eastern Cherokee band, which now occupies the Qualla Reservation located around the village of Cherokee, North Carolina, on the eastern slope of the Smoky Mountains.

The Indians were held in the stockades during the summer of 1838, because the Army thought it was too hot to march. They waited until October, but by then it was too cold, and sadly, the Indians had no choice in the matter. The 1,200 mile, overland trek required six months of walking during the worst of weather conditions. The march took the lives of an estimated 4,000 Cherokees, about one-fourth of their entire population. This tragic march of the Cherokee Indians from their homeland came to be known as the "Trail of Tears."

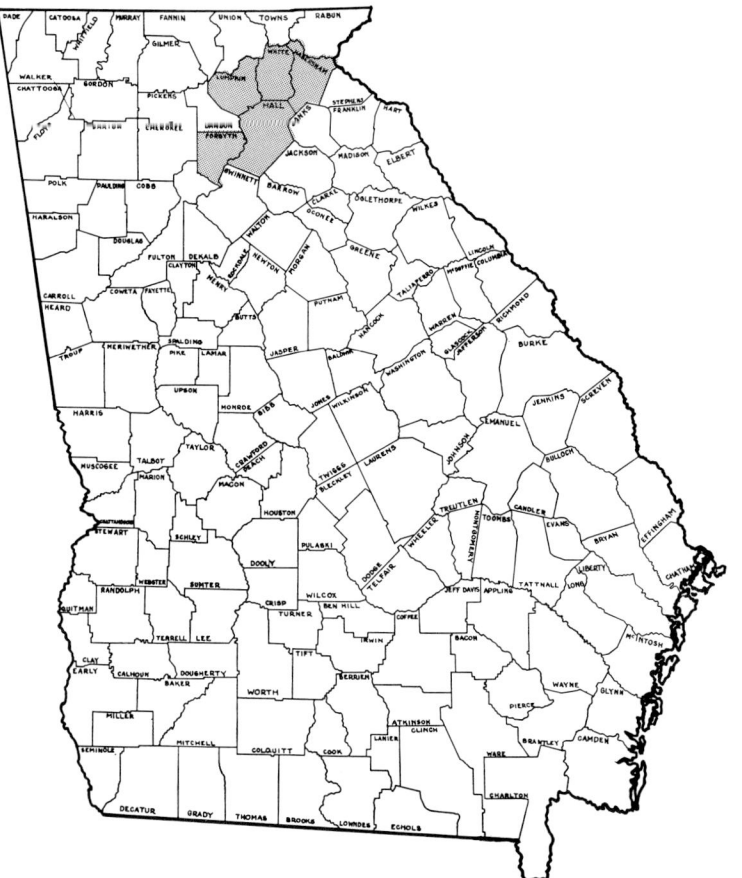

The shaded areas at left show the northeast Georgia counties of Habersham, Hall, Lumpkin, Forsyth and White.

Georgia And Her Counties

Georgia is the largest state east of the Mississippi River having 58,910 square miles. One of the original thirteen colonies, it became a state on January 2, 1788. Georgia boasts a rich and varied history and with 159 counties has more than any other state except Texas. After 1800 land selection and distribution was by lottery. The land lottery gave every qualified Georgian an equal chance to obtain new land. Georgia was the only state that distributed the public domain in this manner.

The geographical areas most discussed in this book are a part of the Blue Ridge Mountains and the gently rolling hills which are a part of the northeast Piedmont. The Blue Ridge is the main range of the Appalachian Mountains in Georgia. The largest river in the area is the Chattahoochee, while the largest lake is Lake Sidney Lanier (man made). Throughout northeast Georgia the reddish colored soil is most often referred to as Georgia Red Clay. Pine and hardwood trees are most commonly found in parts of the Piedmont, with birch, hickory, maple and a variety of oak trees found in parts of the Blue Ridge.

During the nineteenth and early twentieth century Georgia was largely an agricultural state; but by the middle of this century, manufacturing activity was growing. World War II brought many changes to the state. Large numbers of farmworkers left rural areas to take defense jobs in cities, where many of them stayed after the war. By 1950 the United States census reported that, for the first time, more Georgians worked in industry than in agriculture. In 1960, again, for the first time, the census reported that more Georgians lived in the state's urban areas than in its rural areas. Today, Georgia's industries are very diversified.

Agriculture is still very important in Georgia, accounting for a variety of her titles. Earlier in her history, Georgia was known as the "Empire State of the South," but more recently the "Peach State," the "Poultry Capital of the World," and the "Goober State," for its enormous production of peaches, poultry, and peanuts.

Northeast Georgia is becoming more attractive to industry and business as transportation improves and more newcomers move into the area. More people are buying property and retiring in this section of the State. Tourism is also developing as a major business. As growth and progress evolve, the legacy left by those who carved the Northeast Georgia counties of Habersham, Hall, Lumpkin, Forsyth, and White from the wilderness that was the Georgia hills will long be remembered. Their faith in themselves and ability to provide for their own needs through hard work and determination, abiding faith in God, and love for their neighbor are still visible in the area today. It is a rich heritage to be used, contributed to by the present generation, and passed on to the next generation.

Habersham County

Established 1818   County Seat - Clarkesville

Approximately 1949, looking across the Clarkesville Square toward the Habersham County Courthouse which was built circa 1900. After partially burning in 1928, it was remodeled and used once more. Reeves Hardware and Furniture Store is on the left. (Georgia Department of Archives and History).

Habersham County was created by the Georgia Legislature in 1818. It was created from the Cherokee Cessions of 1817, and 1819, and was thirty-one miles long and twenty-three miles wide containing 713 square miles. The County was named for Joseph Habersham, a leader during the Revolutionary War, Postmaster General under President George Washington, and Mayor of Savannah. In 1823 the county seat was chartered and named for the Revolutionary General and Georgia Governor John C. Clark (1819-1823). Habersham originally included parts of White, Stephens, and Rabun Counties.

Hall County

Established 1818   County Seat - Gainesville

Gainesville circa 1910, looking south across the public square. The Hall County Courthouse can be seen in the background. Located on South Bradford Street, it was built in 1883. The courthouse was destroyed by the tornado which struck the city on April 6, 1936. (Georgia Department of Archives and History).

Hall County was created in 1818 by the Georgia Legislature. Once created, the land was distributed by lottery. The county was named for Dr. Lyman Hall, signer of the Declaration of Independence, and later Governor of Georgia in 1783. Three years after Hall County had been chartered, in 1821, Gainesville was incorporated as its county seat. Gainesville was named for General Edmund P. Gaines. It is said that John V. Cotter, a Justice of the Inferior Court in Hall County, suggested the name of Gainesville in honor of General Gaines, having served under him in the War of 1812.

Streetcars, originally pulled by horses, first made their appearance in Gainesville in 1874. The tracks ran from the Southern Railway depot on Main Street to the public square. The first streetcars to run on electric rails were seen in 1903. The streetcar did not have a long life in Gainesville. During the 1920's some of the tracks were removed, and by the late 1940's the balance were removed, leaving the romance with the streetcar as only a fleeting memory of another time.

By the late 1800's the North Georgia Mountain towns were becoming more accessible, thanks to the railroad. Gainesville became the market city for the area. The city was almost completely destroyed by a tornado in 1936. Deaths, injuries, and damage were very high, but Gainesvillians were determined and strong-willed in the face of the disaster. With the help of her friends, Gainesville was rebuilt and continues to grow.

Lumpkin County

Established 1832

County Seat - Dahlonega

April, 1929, looking across the public square at the Lumpkin County Courthouse, in Dahlonega. Notice that the roads are unpaved. The steeple in the background is part of North Georgia College. (Georgia Department of Archives and History).

Lumpkin County was created from land that had been a part of the Cherokee Nation. It was organized by an act of the Georgia Legislature on December 3, 1832, and named for Wilson Lumpkin, Congressman, U. S. Senator, and Georgia Governor (1831-1835). After considerable discussion, Dahlonega was named as the county seat in 1833.

With the discovery of gold near Duke's Creek and the Chestatee River in 1828, hordes of men bearing picks and shovels pushed their way into the Cherokee Nation. By 1832 all Cherokee holdings would be given away to lucky number holders. Nathaniel Nuckolls opened a small hotel in 1832, and soon a settlement sprang up around it called "Nuckollsville." In 1833 a post office was established, and Nuckollsville became Auraria. It is estimated that in 1833 at least 10,000 white people were in Lumpkin County, plus the Indian population. There were some twenty stores, at least a dozen law offices, and numerous other businesses. Auraria felt that, by all rights, she should become the county seat of the new county; but, because of a legal dispute over the ownership of the land upon which the courthouse was to be built, Auraria lost the bid. Dahlonega was more centrally located and had land ready for use. Thus in 1833, the Inferior Court of Lumpkin County gave Dahlonega her new name and title. In 1836 Lumpkin County's new brick courthouse was completed, and the once-thriving mining town of Auraria became nothing more than memories.

Dahlonega, on the other hand, showed such growth, that in 1835 the U. S. Government authorized a mint for the stamping of gold coins. It was offically opened in 1838, and operated until 1861, when it closed at the beginning of the Civil War. In 1871 the mint building was donated to the newly founded North Georgia Agricultural College. The building was destroyed by fire in 1878. The Administration Building for present day North Georgia College stands on the original foundation of the old mint.

Porter Springs

Tucked away in the hills of Lumpkin County was a popular resort known for its healing mineral and freestone waters. It, like numerous other mountain resorts, flourished around the turn of the century. The resort was known as "Porter Springs" or "Queen of the Mountains," at Porter Springs, Georgia. The following is taken from a brochure describing their offerings.

Where Shall I Go This Summer?
To The "Queen Of The Mountains"

No place south of Asheville, N.C., affords such attractions to people desiring to throw off the cares and anxieties of the business world and spend the Summer in the quiet enjoyment of the beauty and grandeur of Nature as PORTER SPRINGS. It is situated one mile from the top of the Blue Ridge Mountains, Lumpkin County, Ga., 29 miles from Gainesville. The pleasure grounds of the hotel property consist of about twelve hundred acres of land, with pleasant, shaded walks and drives through the valleys below and up the peaks above, giving variations of altitude in these pleasant walks and drives on the premises of about one thousand feet.

Mineral and Freestone Waters

There are a great many springs in the cove of the mountain where the hotel is situated; some very strong Chalybeate water, and others pure freestone. From the time of the discovery of these Chalybeate springs in 1868, up to the present time, the medical virtue of the water has been demonstrated every Summer by very remarkable cures. During all these years invalids have flocked to the "Queen of the Mountains" because advised by their physicians of the characteristic difference between Chalybeate water and Sulphur water, or Saline water of any kind. Chalybeate water effectually eradicates all impurities from the blood, acts promptly on the urinary organs, and speedily cures all kidney diseases, dyspepsia, and all diseases of malarial origin; and by virtue of its tonic properties, is specially beneficial in reinvigorating the system after depletion from any cause. To sufferers from overwork, nervous diseases, insomnia, etc., Chalybeate water, with the ozone of the mountains, always rapidly restores wasted vitality.

It is a rare thing to find such combination of water, altitude, climate, and scenery as that found at Porter Springs, and yet to that is added a good table, comfortable quarters and low rates of board-$30.00 per month (4 weeks), $10.00 per week, and $2.00 per day; children under 12, and colored servants in servants' quarters, half rates. We have a herd of thoroughbred Jerseys, which supply milk and butter for the hotel.

Hacks (an open, horse drawn buggie or carriage, which would transport several people) going up leave depot at Gainesville every Tuesday, Thursday and Saturday on arrival of morning train from Atlanta, about 4 o'clock, and will call for passengers at any hotel or boarding house in Gainesville. The hacks going down to Gainesville leave Porter Springs every Monday, Wednesday and Friday, connecting with vestibule train about 2:30 p.m. The hack fare is $2.00; children under 12 years of age half price. Trunks $1.00; valises 25 cents; same each way.

Forsyth County

Established - 1832 County Seat - Cumming

Present Forsyth County Courthouse.

Forsyth County was created on December 3, 1832. It was one of ten counties formed from the old Cherokee County which was actually the Cherokee Nation. The county was named for John Forsyth, a very prominent statesman who served as U. S. Senator, U. S. Secretary of State, Attorney General, and Governor of Georgia (1827-1829).

The county seat was incorporated in 1834. Historians disagree over which of two men the town was named. One was thought to be William Cumming of Augusta, Georgia, and the other Rev. Frederick Cumming of Wilkes County.

Buford Dam which created Lake Sidney Lanier is located in Forsyth County, near the Gwinnett County Line. The Dam was completed by the U. S. Corps of Engineers in 1957.

White County

Established 1857   County Seat - Cleveland

White County Courthouse as it appeared in 1987. This is the original courthouse building completed in 1860 and is said to have been paid for with Confederate money.

Prior to its creation, White County had been a part of Habersham County. On December 22, 1857 the Georgia Legislature passed legislation to create the new county, thanks in large part to the efforts of David T. White of Newton County, for whom most historians say the county was named. However, some say the county was named for Col. John White of Savannah. Col. White fought honorably in the Revolutionary War, but few believe the county was named for him.

In 1820 a post office was established in the settlement of Mt. Yonah. The name was changed from Mt. Yonah to Cleveland, when it became the county seat of White County. Cleveland was named for Benjamin Cleveland who was a State Representative and Senator from Habersham County. White County is also known as the "Gateway to the Mountains."

Hills, Valleys, Country Roads And Mountain Streams

The North Georgia Mountains — where valleys bordered with rolling hills and mountains echo the musical sounds of tumbling rivers and streams — where hidden dirt roads winding through tall oaks and pines extend an invitation to come away and see what wonderous things God hath made. Come listen to the mountains.

Hills, Valleys, Country Roads And Mountain Streams

Come and behold the ritual of Nature as she changes the mountains from lush greens to blazing oranges, reds, yellows and golds. Then, the barron browns and grays can become shining crystal or delicate white softness with new fallen snow.

Hills, Valleys, Country Roads And Mountain Streams

All become a prelude to the glorious celebration of rebirth and new life, which burst forth in bright new colors that are Spring!

Life Was Simpler

The lifestyles of the people who lived in the foothills of the northeast Georgia mountains during earlier days, comes to life through legend, tradition, recorded history and photographs. All these elements have been handed-down from generation to generation. No phase of life has gone unchanged over the years. Some young people today have little idea of how life was lived and of the good and bad times the folks of yesteryear shared. It is often helpful to look back upon the lives of our ancestors and to learn from them.

In the days before there were modern conveniences and so many ways to be entertained, folks in the mountains created their own entertainment. The farmers had "get-togethers" for farm work when extra help was needed. A community gathering could do in one day what it would take a single family weeks to complete, plus socializing with neighbors made it enjoyable; sometimes even fun. Leisure time was rare in those days, so whenever possible, folks would turn "a working" into a special treat. A neighborly corn-shucking could fill the farmer's crib; a log-rolling could clear new land for spring planting; and the barn-raising provided badly needed extra space or help to the neighbor who was just starting his farm. While the men worked, the women usually prepared enough food to satisfy the large crowd. The children helped wherever they were needed, always managing to squeeze in a little play with their chores.

The only heat families had during the winter months came from the wood stove and the fireplace. Even during the day, the house was not very warm, since most houses had cracks in the floor and walls.

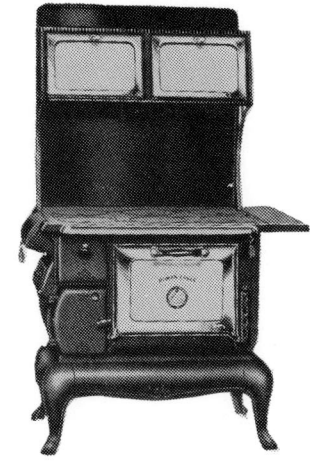

Some houses were poorly built or so old that there were drafty holes throughout. Even well-built houses were cold during the winters, because of poor building materials and lack of heating. At night, the fires were allowed to die down, so the only hope of staying warm was to have five or six quilts on each bed. Large families needed many quilts to get through the winters. Often, a quilt was a work of art, requiring many hours of tedious stitching and preparation of materials; but, because of the urgency of need, the full potential and abilities of the person making the quilt were never seen. However, mothers and grandmothers did put many long hours into making a special quilt for each child to be given as a wedding gift. This was a tradition in most families.

To speed the quilting process along, the women would organize "quilting bees," going from house to house, spending a day at each working on a quilt. It was fun to catch up on all the community gossip and to enjoy a good meal. Also, working together, the women could complete weeks of work in one day. The quilt tops showed their creativity. There were many patterns to select from, and using scraps of material, which had been saved for months, the women created many colorful designs. Today many of these quilts are considered heirlooms and are handed down from one generation to another.

To have a quilting bee, space had to be made in the house to set up the quilt frame, and a bench or chair was needed for each of the ladies to sit around it. A standard-size quilt was about seventy-two by ninety inches. The top of the quilt was usually made in squares, and often, when a quilt was made as a gift, each woman would embroider her name and the date on a square to show her contribution.

The young people of the communities enjoyed doing things together as a group. During the summer, they walked to revival services at night. The roads were dirt, and there were no lights in the country, except maybe a lantern, or in later years, a flashlight. It was not uncommon to walk for several miles to neighboring churches. Singings were also very popular. Usually they were held in the homes of neighbors who owned a piano or an organ. Folks would come from miles around to the Saturday night singings. Sometimes a "pound supper" would be held at someone's home or at the school, and everyone took a pound of food to the supper. When money was needed for a school or church project, the community would have a box supper. This was especially popular with teenage boys and girls. Each girl would prepare a box of food with her name inside the box. No one was supposed to know which box belonged to whom, but usually the word got out. The box suppers were auctioned off to the highest bidder, usually a boy who liked a certain girl. During the meal, the boy then sat with the girl, whose box he had bought.

Candy-pullings were always fun and gave the boy and girl a chance to hold hands, even if they were sticky, greasy hands. The candy was made from cane syrup after it was cooked to just the right consistency. A boy and a girl greased their hands with butter and pulled the hot candy between them until it was light in color. It was then twisted and laid on a smooth surface until it hardened.

There were no firecrackers available to most boys, so they made their own fireworks. They collected whatever cloth scraps their mothers could spare, or would not miss. They rolled the cloth into balls and soaked them in kerosene. At night, they set them on fire and threw the balls from one to another. The boy who could handle the ball fast never burned his hands. Usually there were no severe burns from this activity.

Trees were plentiful on most farms and offered a great opportunity to show off one's skills as a climber. Often, this skill was put to good use by brothers and sisters during arguments and fights. Sometimes, the only way to save your hide was to be able to climb higher than your pursuer.

Although there was little money for Christmas gifts, the season was especially anticipated and enjoyed by young people. They would sometimes walk through the community singing Christmas carols, and some families would serve refreshments, such as parched peanuts, popcorn, popcorn balls, and syrup candy. But "serenading" had an entirely different meaning to young people in earlier days. Christmas was the time for serenading, but it was also the time for all kinds of tricks to be played on everyone in the community. From all accounts, it seems that adults expected this kind of behavior, and for the most part, they accepted it as an unavoidable part of life.

Life Was Simpler

During several interviews for this book, some of the fondest memories related were those of serenading with friends. Most pranks were carried out after dark. It was easier if the folks were already in bed asleep, but not as much of a challenge. The following is a list of some vividly-remembered pranks:

- *A common trick involved going to one man's barn, taking his mule or cow, and swapping it with another man's stock.*

- *One man had a one-horse wagon in his barn. The boys disassembled the wagon and set it "astraddle" the eves of his house. The next day the boys would go back after it was over — not telling the man that they had taken his wagon apart to begin with — and help him get it down.*

- *One really cold night, a group got a bucket of water from the well and tied it over a man's door. One boy knocked on the door, told the man he had a flat tire, and asked if he could come and help change it. The man pushed the screen door open, and the bucket of cold water fell on him. Of course, then, the boys were nowhere to be seen.*

- *One farmer in the community had two mules that were so thin you could see their ribs. The boys painted the mules with black and white paint to make them look like zebras.*

- *A group of boys decided to serenade one particular family in their community. They waited until late at night when the family was ready for bed. The fire in the stove had died down, so they went up on the roof and stuffed "tow-sacks" into the flu of the chimney. The boys knew the family's routine for getting up and dressing for work. They also knew where the man of the family kept his clothes and what he usually wore. They knocked on the door and were invited into the house to visit "a spell." They had a sack of cockleburs they had gathered in the field and hidden under a coat, along with a bottle of Karo syrup. The "carrier" excused himself to the man's bedroom, for some reason, put the burs inside the man's coveralls and poured the Karo syrup into his shoes. The next morning, on schedule, the wife got up first to prepare breakfast and start the fire in the heater. All the smoke came out into the house, because of the sacks in the flu. She didn't know what to do, so she screamed for her husband to come and help her. He quickly jerked on his coveralls and slipped on his shoes, burs, syrup and all! He knew then he had been had. All these inside details were told by the boys later, after the excitement was over.*

- *Another trick was to wait until everyone was asleep, slip up close to the house and then ring cow bells, shoot guns (with shot taken out), and generally make as much noise as possible to wake them up.*

- *Occasionally, a man's wagon wheel would be taken off his wagon and then wedged onto the top of a small tree that had been pulled over. The tree was then turned loose, and there was the man's wagon wheel several feet up in the air. Considerable effort had to be used to get it down.*

The pranks were never meant to hurt anyone and for the most part never did.

Also at Christmas, most children hung a stocking on the mantle for Santa to leave a treat. The only gifts some children received would be one or two apples and oranges, some peppermint candy sticks, and sometimes a coconut, or nuts. Some children would get a small toy, while others never received a toy for Christmas during their entire childhood. There were families who had a Christmas tree, which they cut in the woods and decorated with homemade decorations. Other families never decorated their homes for the holidays. Most families did have a better than normal meal on Christmas Day, and usually only the essential chores had to be done. It was one of a very few days during the year on which some farm families did not work, while for others, it was their only day off, except for Sundays.

Square dancing was popular in the early days. It was the only kind of dancing done by most. The closest a boy came to a girl (in public) was to hold her hand at arm's length as the calls were sung. The only place to have a dance was at someone's house in the community. The biggest bedroom in the house was usually the room used. The men would "tear down" (take apart) all of the furniture and move it to another room. The musicians, usually playing banjos and violins, would be in one corner of the room, and the rest of the room was used for dancing. Afterwards, everyone helped put the furniture back together and moved it back where it belonged. To some, square dancing was a fun way to spend a Saturday night, while to others, it was against their religious beliefs, as was drinking alcoholic beverages.

In the late 1920's and early 1930's, two wonderous inventions began appearing in some of the homes throughout the mountains of Georgia! The families who were fortunate enough to own either of these two items quickly became the families to be with every Saturday night. The crystal battery radios came to the small mountain communities long before electricity plugged them into the outside world. Many of the mountain folks never traveled farther than ten or twenty miles, at most, from their homes. But the radio allowed them to take their first journey to far-away places and to hear things they had never heard before. By today's standards the distances were not that great; but then, the places might just as well have been in another world, because those folks sitting beside their radios could not get there. The old radios had names such as the RCA Radiola and the Atwater Kent. Radio logs were kept of stations that were listened to, because to find the station again, required knowing the call letters, the wave length, and making from three to five dial settings. WSM in Nashville, Tennessee, and WCKY in Cincinnati, Ohio, were two much listened-to stations. The most popular program in the community was the Grand Old Opry, broadcast by WSM. The prize fights also had many loyal listeners. A member of one family owned a truck in the 1930's that he used in his one-man dirt hauling company. The family did not own a radio for their house, but his truck had a radio in it. So, every Saturday night, the neighbors came over, and he pulled the truck up to a raised window, turned on the radio, and everyone enjoyed listening to the Grand Old Opry. Improvising and finding ways to make the most of what you had was nothing new to people in those days.

The other treasured new addition to some homes was the Victrola, the first phonograph. To make it play, someone had to generate power by turning a hand crank. This first phonograph played a cylinder disk to make music. One that played the 78 rpm, flat record was soon available; but the recordings had a "tinny sound." To the folks who had little music in their lives, other than at church, the records must have sounded heavenly. It was an exciting time when a new record was brought home! Family and friends would gather around the Victrola to listen as the record was played over and over again. Traveling salesmen sold the Victrolas, along with many other items, going from house to house through the communities. The Victrola could also be ordered from Sears, Roebuck for around $15, as could almost anything else the farm family might need. If the Sears, Roebuck and Company Catalogue did not carry the items needed, there was always the Montgomery Ward Catalogue.

The passage of the 18th Amendment to the Constitution of the United States, forbidding the manufacturing, sale, or transportation of alcoholic beverages, brought about the period known as the "Prohibition Era," from 1920 to 1933. The small farmers in the mountains of northeast Georgia were finding it

Life Was Simpler

difficult to make enough money to buy supplies and equipment for the farm and the necessities needed by their family. It was apparent that cotton was not going to become the big cash crop in the mountains that it had been on the southern Georgia plantations. Small quantities of farm products were grown and sold, some sawmilling was done, and wild huckleberries became a brief cash crop for some families in White County. The huckleberries grew wild in the woods and were picked and sold to a local wholesale grocer who shipped them to various parts of the country. So considering the plight of many mountain folks, the temptation to make and sell the mountain alcoholic drink called "moonshine" or "white lightning," and to make money, was worth the risk of being caught by government or revenue agents.

The "stills" (distilleries) were usually hidden in the mountains near streams. As the number of "bootleggers" grew, the agents became a common sight, roaming the mountains looking for stills. As it grew to be big business for some people, some mountain folks protected their stills with guns. It was against the code of the mountains to report a still to the revenue agents. But it was worth $10 to the person who reported the still, and $10 was hard to come by in those days. The folks who looked for the stills were called "branch walkers," because they walked up and down the branches and creeks looking for signs of stills. They also kept a close eye out for a stream of smoke rising above the tree tops on a mountainside.

During the prohibition era, some of the mountain preachers were known to accept contributions from church members in the form of moonshine. But, as a minister of the gospel, Claude Hood has always strongly believed that one's life speaks louder, and says more, than all of the words one might ever speak. Thus, in his quiet way, without shouting it from the roof tops, he stood against making, selling and drinking moonshine. Some of his friends and a few church members were either large suppliers or enjoyed a drink of moonshine now and again. Some also gave up these habits during this time. He has never been one to condemn people for their actions; he may not agree with the act, but his deep love for those whom he has served never waivered. Because of his sincerity and kindness, even the meanest, most disrespectful people have respected the spirit of the man and have tried to present a good image when in his presence.

For years after the federal law was repealed, moonshine continued to be made in the mountains. Some folks had to serve jail and prison terms for making and selling it. Even when it was so plentiful, Claude was never offered a drink by any member of his churches; however, he can remember staying overnight at the home of one particular church member and hearing the "jugs" being loaded into cars outside his window.

Often people got caught hauling the moonshine to the buyer during the prohibition years. One undertaker was caught hauling it in his hearse. He had filled a casket with jugs and even had a floral arrangement on top of it for authenticity.

Hunting was a big sport for the men and boys. Usually hunting served a dual purpose. It was a fun sport, and it also provided food. Raccoons, possums, squirrels, and rabbits were the normal objects of the hunt. Hunting dogs were helpful anytime, but the fox hunter was especially attached to his dogs.

Hubert Burke was a dedicated hunter. Each of his children had a trained dog for hunting. Edna (right) is standing beside her dog, Bonnie.

Considerable time and money could be spent on the fox hounds and their training. Most fox hunters knew their dogs so well that they could recognize each dog by its bark during a chase, even when it was far away in the woods at night. Fox hunting was different from other types of hunting. It required more training, discipline, and skill. The fox hunt was a game of chase by the man and his hounds. They became a special team.

There was very little waste on a farm. A use could be found for almost everything. The ashes from the fireplace and the kitchen stove were kept in a hopper or container during the winter months to use in making lye soap. The ashes were kept dry until spring and the "right time of the moon" to make soap. When the time was right, water was poured over the ashes. The liquid which drained from the bottom of the container was called "lye." This liquid was placed into an iron washpot. After the amount needed was collected from the ashes, a fire was built under the washpot. Scraps of meat and grease, which had been saved, were put into the pot with the lye. This mixture was boiled for just the right amount of time, being stirred with a wooden paddle. No recipe was used, or needed, by the experienced soap-maker. She knew when the proper amounts had been used and when the right consistency was reached. When the mixture had cooked enough, the fire was put out, and the soap was carefully poured into wooden molds or left to harden in the washpot. By the next morning, it would have hardened. The soap was then cut out of the washpot in chunks, or turned out of the molds, and stored until needed.

A more modern recipe for soap was as follows:

Grandmother's Old Fashioned Soap

2 1/2 pints of water
6 pounds of clean fat
1 13-ounce can of lye

Dissolve lye in cold water. Heat fat until it is clear liquid and cool at room temperature. Pour lye water into fat in a thin stream. Stir slowly in the same direction until the lye thickens. When it reaches the consistency of thick pea soup, pour the soap into molds (milk cartons or wooden boxes lined with wax paper). Leave the soap in the molds undisturbed for at least 24 hours. Some people let their soap cure a week to six weeks before use. This recipe yields approximately nine pounds of soap and costs very little to make.

Life Was Simpler

Lye soap was the only soap available for washing clothes and dishes and for personal hygiene. Washing clothes for a family often was work! An iron wash-pot was filled with water, then heated by building a fire under it. The clothes were beaten with a battling stick (a wooden paddle) to help loosen the dirt and then scrubbed on the "rub board." This was usually a textured piece of tin, enclosed in a wooden frame, with two legs to help support it while in use. For most folks who washed in their back yards, the water had to be drawn from the well; but, when a stream was nearby, some families carried their clothes to the running water. The clothes were then hung on a clothes line or spread over bushes to dry in the sun.

As years passed, progress helped with the weekly wash. The hand-cranked wringer came first and was a tremendous help in not having to wring each piece of clothing by hand, especially the large pieces. Around 1950, electricity brought a washing machine which stood on legs and had an electric wringer which would pull the clothes through. They would then be rinsed in the tin washtubs.

By the time modern washing machines arrived on the scene, people were beginning to expect and demand modern gadgets and conveniences, so, although it was a tremendous improvement, the washing machine did not mean as much to the farm wife as had the earlier small conveniences.

Even in the 1930's, most of the counties in northeast Georgia were still largely agricultural and rural. There were few cars outside the county seats, which were usually the largest towns in each county.

To run for a local public office in White County in the thirties meant "electioneering" or campaigning throughout the county on horseback. The campaign was during the winter months, and snow was on the ground part of the time. The candidate would ride up to the houses and knock on the doors. Usually, he was invited in to warm himself before going to the next house. Each voter had to pay a one-dollar poll tax in the early 1900's before voting. Most women in the area did not vote at the time, even though they were given the right to vote in 1920, with the passage of the 19th Amendment to the Constitution.

News of the state, nation, and the world came slowly to the mountain communities. Some of the families subscribed to the local town paper, usually a weekly, or the Georgia Department of Agriculture's "Market Bulletin." A few folks received the "Atlanta Constitution."

Over the years, White County, along with the neighboring counties, always sent her boys off to fight during the wars. World War II was no different, and as in all wars, some did not return home. The American Red Cross designated one specific person in a county or several counties, to deliver casualty messages to families whose sons or daughters were either killed or wounded. In one such case, the messenger was well-known throughout the area, and it soon became known that he was also the Red Cross' casualty messenger. Families who had sons in service lived in fear of receiving word that their child had been killed. When this man would go to see someone about regular business, if they had a child in service, they would start screaming, as he walked up to the porch, before he could tell them he was not delivering a message from the War Department. He soon learned that he could not go into the county to any soldier's home on business without letting the family know ahead of time that he was coming.

Telling a family of the death of a child was never easy; but, one message he delivered stood out in his mind:

A young soldier, who had been reared by his grandmother, was returning home after serving overseas. He was killed in an automobile accident on his way home from Fort Campbell, in Kentucky. I went to deliver the message to his grandmother. When I got there, people were standing out in the yard and on the porch, so I figured someone had already told her. I walked up to one man and asked where the grandmother was, and he said that she was in the front room, and I should go on in the house. I walked in, and there the grandmother was in a casket. I never had such a funny feeling. I finally found the boy's aunt and gave her the message of his death. It was a terribly sad day for that family.

The days of the Great Depression brought their own kind of sadness to the hills of north Georgia. The farmers may not have lost vast fortunes, as some on Wall Street had; but, having never owned much, materially speaking, they had even less now with the Depression. Times were equally difficult for the merchants and businessmen who lived and worked in the small towns and cities of the mountain region. Many men, who were unable to support their families by farming, could not find any other work in the area. It was not until the Works Progress Administration (WPA) was established, in 1935, that work was provided for persons without jobs. The WPA was a part of "The New Deal" reform program under President Franklin D. Roosevelt. However, many folks felt that the New Deal programs were

Construction of Highway 52, east of Dahlonega, circa 1920. (Georgia Department of Archives and History)

just handouts and charity. They believed it was wrong to accept government payments of any kind. One man did not recall what his starting salary was with the WPA, but he did remember getting a raise to twenty-four cents an hour. He worked building new roads in the area, repairing old ones, and building bridges. The only tools the workers had were a pick (mattock) and shovel. Two men would work together on one job, taking turns using the pick and shovel. One would use the pick and slope the bank for two hours, while the other man shoveled the dirt. They would then swap jobs. When top soil was to be loaded in the soil pit, it would take six men using shovels three minutes to load a dump truck. The new roads would be surveyed and stakes set, then the crews would come along and build the new road, almost entirely with manpower alone, since very little machinery was available.

Life Was Simpler

In the early days, the roads were used only for wagons, a few carriages, and for walking. As the automobile became more popular in later years, the need for better roads increased. In the early days it was a common practice to swap work on the roads for property taxes owed by the land owner. Whether he did not have the money, or wanted to keep what he had, he or his older sons would often work on the roads for a prescribed number of days. This was one way that the county was able to repair the roads, as very little money was available for this purpose.

It might be said that clothing was somewhat drab. Men's suits came in one color, basic black, with an accompanying white shirt. Women might have a little more color in their Sunday clothes, but work clothes were very basic. It was more important then that clothes be durable and serviceable than how they looked. However, folks still liked to get dressed up, just as they do today.

A sawmill crew that worked for Hubert Burke of Habersham County. Circa 1930.

Photography was one of the greatest inventions to help record and preserve memories of events and people. Treasured heirlooms were now possible to the rich or poor. In the late nineteenth and early twentieth centuries, few folks in the rural areas of Georgia owned cameras, but this did not stop them from loving photographs of themselves and their families. Photography studios were usually located in larger towns. However, if the family could not get to town, they were not out of luck. There were traveling photographers who went door-to-door throughout rural communities making pictures of families at their homes. Sometimes pictures were shot outside, or the photographer might provide a backdrop to give the affect of being in a studio. Most of the time folks dressed in their Sunday best, but occasionally pictures were taken of them in their everyday work clothes.

It was a big event to get a "store bought" dress, suit, or pair of shoes! Because there was very little money, most clothes were handmade by the women of each family. They were made more for service than looks. Usually boys got one or two pairs of overalls each year. Shirts, dresses, and underwear were often made from flour or chicken feed sacks. These cloth sacks had printing on them, and it had to be scrubbed off the material before being sewn into clothes. The printed and plain feed sacks were used to make dresses and aprons. Shirts were made from the solid blue sacks, with white sacks being used for underwear, sheets, and towels. Prints were used for curtains and table cloths. When it could be afforded, unbleached sheeting was bought by the bolt for sewing. A heavier material called "ducking" was used for tablecloths, curtains, and cotton picking sacks. A store-bought collar, lace or other trimming would make a homemade dress look prettier, and folks were proud of Sunday-go-to-meeting clothes. Clothes, until they were worn out, were passed down from older to younger children.

Before store-bought dye was available, people made their own dye from barks, red clay, and vegetables. Shoes were not worn by some children until after the first frost. Some children were fortunate enough

Dressed In Style

Garland Dixon ca. 1900. Habersham Mills Village behind him.

Cora Harrison Dixon.

Pearl Dixon (right) and a friend.

Carrie Dixon (right) and Ruth Allen.

Lessie Dixon (right) and Odessa Highlove.

Dressed In Style

Good friends, (l-r) Tom McEntire, Edgar Pardue, Hubert Burke, and Jim Shirley.

Best friends, (l-r) Dessie Pardue, Lillie Burke, and Mrs. Tom McEntire.

Garnett Sosebee from Habersham County served in World War I.

Wiley Hood (right) and brother, G. Claude Hood. Most all men's clothes were black in the early 1900's.

to get a pair of "Polly Parrot" shoes to wear to school and to church, while others had to make do with a more uncomfortable shoe made from hard leather. They required considerable wear before they were "broken-in" enough to stop hurting the feet, and this seemed to take forever.

Owning a "union suit" or a pair of "long johns" saved many a life, or so it was thought. Life on a farm required a lot of work out-of-doors. Additionally, most homes, schools, and churches were poorly heated; therefore, the added warmth provided by a union suit made it a welcomed addition to any wardrobe.

A necessity to farm women was their apron. Covering most of their dress, it served many purposes. Not only did it protect their clothes from getting dirty, but it was also used as a carrier or handy pouch. The bottom of the apron would be held up and stove wood, fruits, vegetables, eggs, and many other items could be carried in it during the course of the day.

Lillie Burke (Edna's grandmother), age 93, shows off her apron which is similar to the ones worn by farm women earlier in the century.

Constant concerns to mothers who had children in school were the childhood diseases and insects caught at school and brought home. Insects called lice were common during the early part of the century. They were usually found in the hair, thus they were referred to as "head lice." Mothers might try to pick or comb them out of the hair, being sure that they got all of the "nits" (eggs) out too. One remedy to try to kill lice was to pour kerosene over the hair, while a more extreme method was to shave the child's head!

One of the biggest problems of having a large family was keeping the entire family from catching diseases from each other. With so little knowledge of the causes of many illnesses, and even less knowledge of cures, minor illnesses to us today were often life-threatening in earlier years. It was possible for an entire family to be killed by a flu or measle epidemic or other diseases. So although some methods to treat and cure illnesses and injuries sound strange today, they were usually the best and only medicines available at the time. This is why great faith was placed in these remedies. Even after the country doctors began to hang out their shingles in the towns of the north Georgia mountains, lack of money and transportation were still handicaps in seeking treatment. From today's perspective, looking back at some of the remedies used and the results, can make for some good story telling.

Such a story is about one mother's efforts to rid her children of the dreaded itch. As with the lice the itch was of little concern to some families, while to others it was not a disgrace to catch, but it was a disgrace to keep. With this thought in mind, no suggested cure was too extreme to try. The itch would cause a rash to break out between the fingers, on the arms, and other parts of the body, and the itching did not stop. It has been said that no one ever knew what finger nails were made for, until they've had the itch! Sulfur and lard mixed together was one tried and true remedy; but, sometimes it worked very slowly. A rumor in one community said that a great new cure for the itch was to boil pokeberry root in water and use it as a bath. The itch had been contracted by the two eldest boys of a family who lived back in the woods at the foot of a mountain. The mother, having heard of the pokeberry root cure, had a bath prepared for them in the back bedroom when they came home from school one afternoon. The oldest son was called to come and soak in the tub first. So the boy reluctantly stepped into the tub and sat down. Faster than you could blink an eye, he was out of that tub, tore the door open, and up the side of that mountain he ran, naked as a jay bird! You could hear him yelling as he ran. The pokeberry juice was about to burn him up! The mother, not being one to give up at first try, turned to the other son and said, "Well, he ain't got a lick of sense anyhow, you get in the tub." Having the same firey result, the second boy "passed" his brother about half way up that mountain!

By the time the boys had stopped burning and came down the mountain, their mother had decided the pokeberry root water wouldn't work if she couldn't keep the boys in it, so she mixed up a batch of sulfur and lard and greased all of the children from top to bottom. The second son recalls, "You couldn't stay in the bed, 'cause you kept sliding out from between the sheets, right down to the foot of the bed! We had to do this for three days and three nights. Every morning there'd be three or four of us piled up at the foot of the bed, naked as jay birds, greased in sulfur and lard. We finally got rid of the itch, but it may have been because of the odor from the sulfur and lard, 'cause it smelled terrible!"

Another insect that was a pest at this time was the bedbug. They infested the bedstead, mattress, and linens. While their victims slept, the bedbugs attacked by biting them. Having bedbugs did not bother some families, but to others it was disgraceful, and drastic measures were taken to keep a house free of them. Bedbugs were also called "chinches." Sometimes they were brought into a house on visitors' clothes. One method used to keep the bug away from the beds was to fill fruit jar lids with lamp oil and set the bedpost in the lids. The bugs could not jump or swim across the oil to the bed. There were no exterminators to call or sprays to buy to kill them. So, the only way to get rid of them was to take the beds completly apart and move them outside where they were washed in boiling water and lye soap or turpentine. All the bed linens had to be washed in hot water and then placed in the sun to dry. The bedbugs remaining in the cracks and crevices of the furniture had to be picked-out by hand.

It seems that everything had to be tough and durable in the early days in order to survive; people, clothes, houses, and furniture. Most all farm houses had wooden floors, and most of these floors in the northeast Georgia mountains were cleaned with dirt, "white dirt," that is! This white dirt was very special. There seemed to be a vein of white dirt that ran along the banks of the creeks and branches of the area. It was dug out, carried to the houses, and spread over the floors. It was spread over the kitchen floor to help absorb the grease spills during the week; then before Sunday, it was swept out. The dirt would be spread over the floors throughout the house and left for two or three days, and as it was walked over it scrubbed the floors. The white dirt was not like plain dirt, because it acted as a mild bleaching agent on the floors. It was more like soapstone, and in early summer, when folks no longer needed heat, it was mixed with a little water and used to whitewash the fireplace. It was also common to whitewash the tree trunks during the summer months. A little lime was mixed with the white dirt and water, and the tree trunk was painted from the ground about half way up the trunk.

Brooms were made from broom straw or shucks. The broom straw grew in open fields and was gathered and cleaned, then tied together and made to the most accommodating lengths for the users. Toothbrushes were made by breaking a small stick from a blackgum tree. The end of the stick was spread out until it looked like a little brush. The brush was wet, dipped into a mixture of soda and salt, and then used to brush the teeth.

Country Homes

An early log cabin. To avoid a possible fire, the kitchen would sometimes be detached from the house. The "paling fence" was used to keep out unwanted animals. It was also used to protect the garden.

Fred Hood stands in the yard of his first home in 1935, on Town Creek in White County.

Country Homes

Farm house on Mossy Creek in White County. Most houses of this era had front and back porches. During the summer many chores were done on the porch, because it was cooler. Notice the kitchen at the back of the house (right).

The home of Boyd Hunt (deceased), who taught school for many years. Located in the Mt. View Community, White County.

Country Homes

In the Mossy Creek District of White County is the house where Claude Hood's grandparents lived, Mr. & Mrs. J. Mood Allison.

In Lumpkin County, the Allen Dyer Homeplace, on Porter Springs Road, now stands in disrepair. During his early ministry, Claude was an overnight guest in this house.

Life Was Simpler

There was no such thing as insurance to rural folks. If bad luck struck, the only help available was from friends and neighbors. Although very independent, families were also very interdependent upon each other. The finishing touch on any farm house was a lightning rod. Whether they served the purpose for which they were sold was not at question, they made a statement to the neighbors and all who passed by; the family who lived there was prosperous enough to afford a lightning rod.

In the early days of the automobile a license was not needed to operate it. Anyone who could learn to drive, or thought they could drive, could take to the open road. In 1937, the General Assembly passed a law creating the Drivers License Bureau for the State of Georgia. Individual licenses were obtained by writing and requesting a license from the Bureau. In 1939, the law required the applicant to go to the Bureau for an eye, written and road exam. By 1940, a family plan license was available to the heads of households for $1.00, which entitled him to buy his wife's license for 50 cents, and a license for any minor child over 16 years of age for 25 cents. The price also included the eye, written, and road exam. Changes in operating regulations have continued to be made as the number of automobiles have increased.

When travel was on foot or by wagon, the trip into town for supplies was only made a few times a year for most folks. But usually there was a small general store in each community. It was to these stores that the wife and children would take their eggs or butter to sell or trade to get a little extra money or small items needed. Occasionally the children might slip one or two eggs to the store for a piece of candy. The store owner knew everybody in the community, and he did a lot of business on credit. When a crop was harvested or the farmer made any money he would be paid. Peddlers also traveled through the country, going door-to-door, selling their wares from packs on their backs. They usually carried cloth, thread, and other items which were of more interest to the women of the house. Later, during the 1930's and 1940's, "rolling stores" became popular. This was a man driving a panel truck traveling through the communities from house to house selling groceries and drygoods. Occasionally he too, would buy or trade for vegetables and eggs.

Not so long ago, "country stores" traded or bartered with local folks to get some of the food they sold. It was the only way many farm families could survive when money was scarce. Eggs were traded most often.

The Old Country Store

The E. B. Hunt General Store on Mossy Creek, White County.

General Store near the Holly Springs Community, Hall County.

In Hall County located on Highway 129, at an intersection near Brookton, was a little country store and service station known as "Quillian's Corner." Today the intersection still bears the same name, although the store is no longer there. (Georgia Department of Archives and History)

Life Was Simpler

In towns some wholesale groceries also sold to retail customers. Every customer required a clerk to serve him because almost everything came in large quantity containers. Sugar, salt, and beans came in 100 pound bags, and lard came in 50 pound containers. The customers had to bring their own container for the lard if they bought less than the full unit. Before refrigeration, the only meats sold were meats preserved with salt, such as fatback or side meat. After a few folks got iceboxes, the stores were able to carry cubed steak. It came in gallon buckets and was fresh meat salted down. It was expensive during the 1920's, but a few people could afford it. Salt herring came in wooden buckets. It was so salty most folks soaked it overnight to get some of the salt out. To soak the fish, a tub was filled with water and the fish placed in it, then corn cobs were placed on top of the fish. The cobs dissolved a lot of the salt overnight. Loaf bread was bought from Aunt Betty's in Gainesville, Georgia. Later, Merita bread became popular. It was made in Cornelia, Georgia.

Before kerosene or electric refrigerators, iceboxes were cooled by blocks of ice which were sold by the "iceman" and delivered to the homes by wagon or truck.

White County butter and huckleberries were shipped as far away as New York and Chicago. During the 1930's as high as 600 gallons of huckleberries were shipped from Cleveland, Georgia. Wagon trains would come across the mountains and bring peas, other vegetables, and fruits, as well as syrup to sell in Cleveland and Gainesville or to put on the train for shipping across the country. J. D. Jewell was just beginning his poultry enterprises in Gainesville. He would accept chicken and eggs on consignment, sell them and then pay for them.

Some of the stores in Cleveland from the early to mid 1900's, were: The Cleveland Grocery, owned by the Mauney family; the Head family owned Head's Grocery; and there was the Telford and Kenimer General Store. In the county there were stores owned by: John D. Cooley, W. I. Stovall, John Stovall, and E. B. Hunt. Most folks who traveled Highway 129 from Cleveland to Gainesville were familiar with Quillian's Corner Grocery and Service Station near Brookton, in Hall County.

Before the automobile, when travel was on foot or in a wagon or carriage, the covered bridge offered the traveler shelter from an afternoon rain. The cover also protected the bridge from the elements allowing it to remain passable in all kinds of weather, and because the actual bridge was not exposed to the elements, it did not decay as rapidly. And not last in importance, many a kiss was stolen by sweethearts traveling through the covered bridge. Most of the covered bridges are no longer in existence, however, there are a few remaining to see and enjoy from a lifestyle of another time.

Stovall Mill Bridge, built in 1895, in the Blue Creek Community of White County. (Georgia Department of Archives and History)

A Country Home

I visited a country home: a modest, quiet house sheltered by great trees and set in a circle of field and meadow, gracious with the promise of harvest. Barns and cribs were filled, and the old smokehouse odorous with treasure; the fragrance of pink and hollyhock mingling with the aroma of garden and orchard, and resonant with the hum of bees and the poultry's busy clucking; inside the house, thrift, comfort, and that cleanliness that is next to Godliness; the restful beds, the open fireplace, the books and papers, and the old clock that had held its steadfast pace amid the frolic of weddings, that had welcomed in steady measure the new-born babes of the family, and kept company with the watchers of the sickbed, and had ticked the solemn requiem of the dead; and the well-worn Bible that, thumbed by fingers long since stilled, and blurred with tears of eyes long since closed, held the simple annals of the family, and the heart and conscience of the home.

Henry W. Grady, 1850-1889

Farming Was A Way Of Life

The life of the farmer has always been a difficult one. The ratio of manhours expended, in relation to volume of return, has never tipped the scales in the farmer's favor. Life was harder for the smaller family farmer, who farmed alone, with only the help of his wife and children. This was the reason for larger families in the early 1900's. In those early days, most of the farmland had to be cleared before it could be farmed; but, in the mountains of northeast Georgia, it was never that simple. Once the land was cleared, the farmer had to fight a never ending battle to keep his land. His constant enemy was Mother Nature. Anything left untended for very long in the mountains was quickly reclaimed by the forces of nature and returned to its natural state of undergrowth, bushes, and trees.

Farming was very simple then, as compared to today's modern farm equipment, soil additives, pest controls, fertilizers, and even computers and enclosed cab tractors, complete with stereos and telephones. The early farmer did everything by hand. He walked down every row, behind his mule or horse, several times during the growing season. Even if he had the property, unless the children were old enough to work like an adult, he could only cultivate the amount of land equivalent to his available manpower. Sometimes, renting part of his land to a tenant farmer for a share of the crops not only helped the property owner, but it helped a family who needed a place to live and a way to make a living.

During the 1800's and early 1900's, the majority of folks in northeast Georgia, earned their livelihood from farming. Some farmers owned richer farmland, some were just better farmers, and many other factors entered into the equation, but very few got rich farming. Since there seemed to be no other way to make any money, some of the farmers made moonshine. To a few, it became a full-time means of support, while to others, it was only an occasional way to earn some extra money when needed.

There were several resorts located in the northeast Georgia mountains during the late 19th and early 20th centuries, but one by one, they slowly closed their doors. Three cotton mill villages were located around the city of Gainesville, in Hall County, Gainesville Mill, New Holland Mill, and Chicopee Mill. The city was also active with other business and trade. The growth, however, did not extend into the county. Since Gainesville was the largest town north of Atlanta, most of the cotton and other farm products were taken there for selling or trading. Habersham County also had a mill village which provided employment and housing for its employees, but this was only a small percent of the total county population. It would be the 1940's and 1950's, before the farmers of northeast Georgia were introduced to their most profitable farm venture, the poultry industry. With industry leaders like J. D. (Jessie) Jewell and others, northeast Georgia rapidly became known as a poultry center. Slowly, other industries began to move into the counties, and life, as it had been around the turn of the century, would never be the same again.

Some families still farmed, but now there were alternatives. No longer was farming the only way to provide for one's family. With the automobile came mobility and opportunities for improvements. Since workers could now live in one community and work in another, the small, isolated communities — in which neighbors were dependent upon each other — were also changing. Life seemed to be improving and changing for the better; but, there was a price to pay for everything. The price was a life of ever-increasing complexity. The simple life was disappearing. Now there were choices and decisions to make about so many things that affected their everyday life. There were noticeable differences in material possessions, company bosses controlled the individual's time, and more consideration was given to moving away from the family farm to be nearer a job.

Today's world has retained very little of the old farm way of life, but its memory must be preserved, because every phase of our ancestors' lives revolved around the farm, its crops, and the livestock. Those who are native to the mountains, or whose ancestors lived there, owe their very existence to the farm family's ingenuity and persistence. Although most were never rich in material possessions, these farmers provided for their family's needs. They possessed a great wealth of non-material things: love and support for one's family; concern and responsibility for one's neighbor and fellow-man; faith in God; dedication to one's church; and lastly, great pride in the fact that their word was their bond. A deal could be made on a handshake. These things could not be bought with money yesteryear, and they cannot be bought today.

A few of the farmers living in the mountains today are still farming with the same equipment and using the same methods as their fathers. This includes plowing with a horse. Claude Hood is one of these men. This summer, at seventy-eight years of age, he had three gardens and a large blueberry patch, numerous fruit trees, strawberries, and grapes under cultivation. The results of his hard work were beautiful vegetables and fruits, which were enjoyed by his family and friends.

Claude was expected to do his part on his parents' farm at a young age. He was five years old when he hoed his first corn, and he still remembers the spanking he got that year because his dad found him asleep between the rows of corn. He learned right away that the field was not the place to sleep. Claude grew up loving to farm, and there have been very few years when he has

Claude and Trigger plowing his garden during the summer of 1987. He has owned the horse for more than fifteen years.

not made a garden. Most years, he has farmed acreage in addition to having a large garden. Some years during his ministry in rural churches, his pay was not adequate to support a family, but he always farmed to subsidize the family budget. Often he grew hay and fescue seed, and raised cattle and broilers for market, while providing most of the family's vegetables, fruit, pork, poultry, beef, milk, butter, and eggs. Sometimes during the summer, after being in weeks of revival meetings, he would be so physically and emotionally drained, that it would require a strong will and mind over body, to take care of the farm chores and the crops. One of his favorite sayings has been, "Sometimes you have to do things you don't feel like doing." But on the other hand, working with the soil and seeing things grow have always been his best therapy. For him, it has been a way to renew his spirit, to keep his body strong, and his mind alert.

In 1956, Claude planted corn on fescue sod as part of an experimental project by the U.S. Department of Agriculture. Pictured (l-r) Lester Stovall, Rudolph Clark, Claude and three others interested in the project. (Soil Conservation Service Photo)

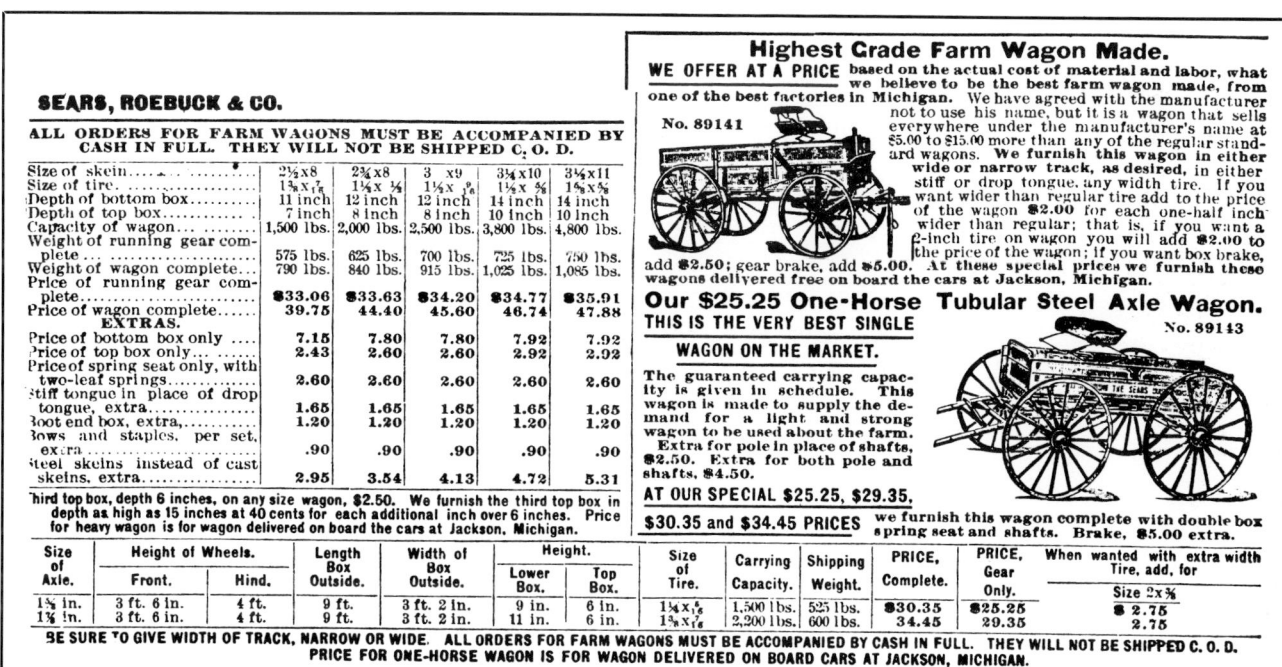

Used by permission.

A poem, by John M. Martin, hangs on Claude's study wall that makes some very true statements about the benefits of farming and gardening:

There's a lot you can do in a garden
Besides raising onions and peas;
It's the place where I know
All alone I can go
To set my distraught mind at ease.
There I dig down
to true understanding;
Resentments I weed at each bed.
And with rake and a hoe
While I'm kneeling I sow
New seeds of forgiveness instead.

There's so much you can do in a garden
Besides pulling up harmful weeds;
On your knees working there
You may think of a prayer
To offer for somebody's needs.

Claude in his garden during the early 1980's.

You can bury your heartaches and anger
Deep under the toughest of sod;
And you'll sweat as you hoe
But you'll certainly grow
In closer communion with God.

There's a lot you can do in a garden
Besides getting healthfully tired;
As you hoe row on row,
Watching everything grow,
With kindlier thoughts you're inspired.
Like a chapel for deep meditation
On weakness and personal strife,
In the garden you feel
As you labor and kneel
Impelled to make more out of life.

* * * * *

Gathering vegetables from his garden, Claude is ready to enjoy some of of the fruits of his labors.

There is much to be remembered about farming in the years gone by. It is interesting that only recently have jogging and walking become popular and said to improve one's health. The farmers of earlier years did not run or walk for pleasure or health. They did both everyday in order to assure they would have the bare necessities of life. It took days, even weeks, to clear new ground and turn it with a two-horse turner. It took even longer, if there was only one horse on the farm. Then a harrow was run over the land to smooth and break up the big clods of dirt. Next came the single-foot plowstock to run a furrow about three feet wide. Some folks liked the rows closer. The farmer was pretty good at plowing a straight row, but if the first row was crooked, the rest would be too.

A well-trained mule or horse easily learned where the plowman wanted him to walk. Even if the rows were laid off in a curved contour, the animal learned to follow the curve of the previous row, though sometimes a "gee" or a "haw" was needed. Some horses and mules just couldn't learn anything, though, and it was always time-consuming to train a young animal where to walk so they wouldn't step on the young plants as they plowed. Usually each farmer had his preference for farming with a horse or a mule. Some said that once a mule learned what to do, he never forgot, but that horses had more sense than mules. A farmer never wanted to trade for mules or horses that had ever run away, so he always asked the horse trader if he knew whether they were "run-away" animals. Mules seemed more prone to do this than horses. This type animal would run away when badly scared; then they lost all reason and became like a wild animal. They could be very dangerous while running. Another good work animal was the ox, which was sometimes cheaper to buy. Oxen were very slow; but they were very strong pulling animals and could work in rougher land than horses or mules. Due to this, oxen were used a lot in sawmilling.

The farmer spent long days with his horse or mule, and they were far easier days if his plow animal and he agreed on what they were trying to accomplish. The farmer communicated to the animal with verbal commands: "whoa," meaning to stop; "gee," the command to go right; and "haw," being the command to go left. He also signaled the horse whether to go right or left through the reins in his hands. The reins were tied to the bridle and bit in the horse's mouth, and a gentle pull on the reins would be felt by the animal, telling it in which direction the plowman wanted it to go. It did not always go in that direction, however. Most farmers were good to their animals, because they knew that they could not earn a living without them.

Wiley Hood on one of his mules, which he used on his farm in the Mt. View Community of White County, during the early 1950's. This picture is also reproduced on the cover.

Before the planter was invented, the farmer had to fertilize and drop each seed by hand. Some innovative farmers invented makeshift devices to drop the seeds faster. The planter was pulled by the horse, just like the plow, and the fertilizer and seed dropped into the row at the same time. There were separate compartments for the fertilizer and the seed, as well as a distance gauge for the dropping of the seed. After the seed was dropped into the furrow, it was covered with dirt by a wheel behind the planter. This one invention saved the farmer many long hours and extra steps.

After the seed came up, the farmer would "run around the corn" and put a furrow down the middle of the row with the McCoy plow. Because of the way the McCoy plow was made, it allowed the farmer to complete his plowing quicker and easier. If the corn got "foul" and too many weeds sprang up, a sweep was sometimes used to go down the middle of the rows and cut the weeds in its path. The corn was usually worked again in about a week and maybe one more time after that. If the farmer didn't have a McCoy plow, a single or double-foot plow was used. It just took longer. Not every child or man made a good plowman. Usually, one or two of the children did all of the plowing, while the others hoed and did other things. To become a plow hand was a big step in getting to be a man.

In the early 1900's, most farmers who lived on the farms in northeast Georgia, thought that their children would become farmers when they grew up, just as they had, and their fathers had. So, the children were taught everything they needed to know to be good farmers. There was an unspoken timetable within most families, which allowed that each male child lived and worked at home until he was twenty-one years old. He was then free to marry, leave home, and work for himself. In the late 1920's and 1930's, the old mold began to break. The children living on the farms began to hear stories of a better way of life in the towns and cities, and the children coming of age during those years began breaking away from the old way of life.

In the early days of farm life, if a neighbor got sick, the community would let their own crops go one day to get together and work the sick neighbor's crops for him. Everybody knew everyone in the community, and generally everything about them, from the color of their horse to the names of all their children. If you did not "fancy" a neighbor's ways, it was usually best to just leave him alone. Some people were a little better off materially than others, but they were not necessarily better people.

Beautiful bottom land, planted for the new growing season. From a distance it looks like a river as it flows through the valley.

When cornmeal was needed, the corn was hauled to the grist mill to be ground to meal. Cotton was taken to the mill to be ginned and was usually sold by the bale in Gainesville or Clermont; but, as a financially profitable farm crop, cotton did not last too long in northeast Georgia. It was hard to get labor to help pick the cotton, and in the early 1920's, the boll weevil arrived, doing great damage to the crops each year.

Some farmers grew wheat on their farms. They sold some of their harvest, but it was grown equally for their own consumption. The grain was taken to the mill to be ground into flour for use at home; usually, a hundred pounds at a time. The families who grew the wheat could count on having good homemade biscuits for breakfast, instead of cornbread, and they had a straw bed "tick" to sleep on. Ticking was what the material was called that was sewn together and stuffed with dried wheat straw to make mattresses for the beds. The straw was usually replaced every year after the wheat was cut. Cotton or feather mattresses were then placed on top of the straw ticks. There were no springs for beds in those days. The wheat was planted in the fall and harvested between May and July. If the weather was good and there was time, the farmer might be able to get in a late crop of peas or corn on the same ground.

The hardest work on the farm may have been cutting or "cradleing" the wheat. Claude's dad did not start growing wheat until Claude was about ten years old. Sometimes they planted as much as twenty acres in wheat. Usually two people worked together when it was time to harvest it. One person would cradle, and the other would bind the wheat into bundles. With one good, strong sweep, half of a bundle could be cut at one time. The binder would follow behind and shock or stack the wheat. Several bundles would be stood together and then capped with two or three bundles, so the water would run off.

"Long about" August, after the wheat had dried, it was taken to the barn for storage.

To get the wheat threshed, the farmers depended on "traveling threshers" to come by their farm. This was a group of men, traveling throughout the hill communities, with the necessary equipment to free the seeds from the straw. Since most farmers did not have any money to pay for the work, the threshers were given room and board and a percent of the wheat they threshed. The grain was stored in a dry place, and as flour was needed, one hundred pounds were usually taken to the mill to be ground. Grist mills were commonly located throughout the communities, so the farmers did not have to travel too far from their homes. The mills had to be located on a stream, because water was needed to turn the paddle wheel to generate the power needed to run the equipment. The corn or wheat was ground between huge, rotating stones.

Most every farmhouse had a GRIER'S ALMANAC hung on a nail beside the fireplace. Every word was read, and much attention was given to the weather forecasts for planning when to plant crops, for canning, and for killing hogs. Many farmers also depended on the signs of the Zodiac listed in the Almanac and on the phases of the moon to help them in deciding when to do their work. Some depended strickly on the signs and would forever declare, it was the only way to farm. Other farmers thought farming by the signs was foolish.

Tanner's Mill, located on the Walnut Fork of the Oconee River in Hall County, is said to be one of the oldest gristmills in this section of the state. It was built after 1823, by David Tanner and his wife Elizabeth. (Georgia Department of Archives and History)

A story is told of a White County farmer who was in the field planting his corn, when one of his neighbors came by, saw what he was doing, and told him that it wasn't the right time of the moon to be planting corn. To which the man planting the corn replied, "I'm not planting my corn on the moon, I'm planting it here in my field."

Those who farmed by the signs said that if corn was planted on the wrong time of the moon, it grew a big stalk and a little ear. Planted at the right time, it produced a good yield on little stalks. Beans planted on the wrong time of the moon would be mostly vines. During the summer when the sap was up, most farmers cut wood for winter on the full of the moon. Cutting at this time drove the sap out, and the wood cured out pretty and white and burned better. It was said that hogs killed on the New Moon produced more lard than hogs killed on the Old Moon. The following are planting tips which Claude has followed for many years when planting his gardens.

Potatoes - Irish
Plant in March when the moon is in Cancer, Scorpio and Taurus. Cut the potatoes in pieces and have at least two eyes in each piece. After planting the potatoes, work them and ridge the soil up some as the vines begin to bloom. Dig the whole patch when the vines die down. Never dig the potatoes when the moon is in the water signs of Cancer, Scorpio, and Pisces.

Onions
Put out onions as early as possible (February). The earlier you get them out, the better they will do. Onion buttons, multiplying or white shallots, or plants may be used. As the onions are worked, dig a little of the dirt away each time. Part of the onion will show, and it will make larger onions. Plant onions when the moon is decreasing in light and is in the earthly signs of Taurus or Capricorn.

Peas - English
Plant peas as early as February. They do not do well when planted late. Frost does not hurt them, and they will not freeze easily. Plant enough seed so that there will be a thick stand when the plants come up. Also, plant in short rows. Plant peas on the New Moon, when the signs are Cancer and Libra.

Lettuce
Plant leaf or head lettuce in early March. Plant in a small bed or corner of the garden. Plant them when the signs are Cancer and Libra.

Turnips
Sow turnip seed twice a year in early spring or early fall. Use the tops (leaves) for greens (turnip greens). To have large turnips, the plants must be thinned. Purple topped or white grow equally well. Plant when the signs are Taurus or Capricorn.

Mustard and Kale
Plant in early spring and late summer. If so desired, the seed may be mixed with the turnip seeds and sown together. Separate rows are easier to identify, however. Plant when the signs are in Cancer or Libra.

Beets
Beets should be planted in February. Sow the seed in quantities that will insure a thick stand of plants. As plants grow, thin as desired, to have larger beets. Plant beets when signs are in Leo.

Cabbage
The Flat Dutch is a favorite variety of cabbage. It needs cool weather and rich soil to grow well. The best times to plant are spring and fall. The gardener may sow the seed or set out plants. Careful attention is required to protect cabbage plants from the cabbage moth, which lays eggs on the leaves. Later these eggs turn into cabbage worms and can completely ruin a crop, if they are not controlled.

The farmer was also very observant of all the signs provided by nature. Being able to know what the weather was going to do was critical to him. There were no advanced, weather forecasting equipment, meteorologists, radio, or television as we have today, to give the farmer advanced warnings of approaching storms, droughts, or freezes. It has always been said that animals have an extra sense of impending danger, or of unusually cold winter approaching. The farmer knew his farm animals, and he learned and respected the wild animals around him. He also paid careful attention to the sky, watching for each change in the sun, moon and stars. A red sky at sunup was a sign of rain, and a red sky at sundown was a sign of fair weather. Hornets would build their nest close to the ground when it was going to be a cold winter and high in a tree when the winter would be warm. If the corn had thick shucks, the winter would be cold. When there was a circle around the moon, it was a sign of rain. The number of stars within the circle told how many days until the rains came. When the cattle stood around the barn, and did not go out into the pasture, bad weather was near. When hogs "toted" sticks to make their beds it would be cold weather. Special attention had to be paid to the horses and mules during a storm to keep them from getting frightened and running away.

Farming Was A Way Of Life

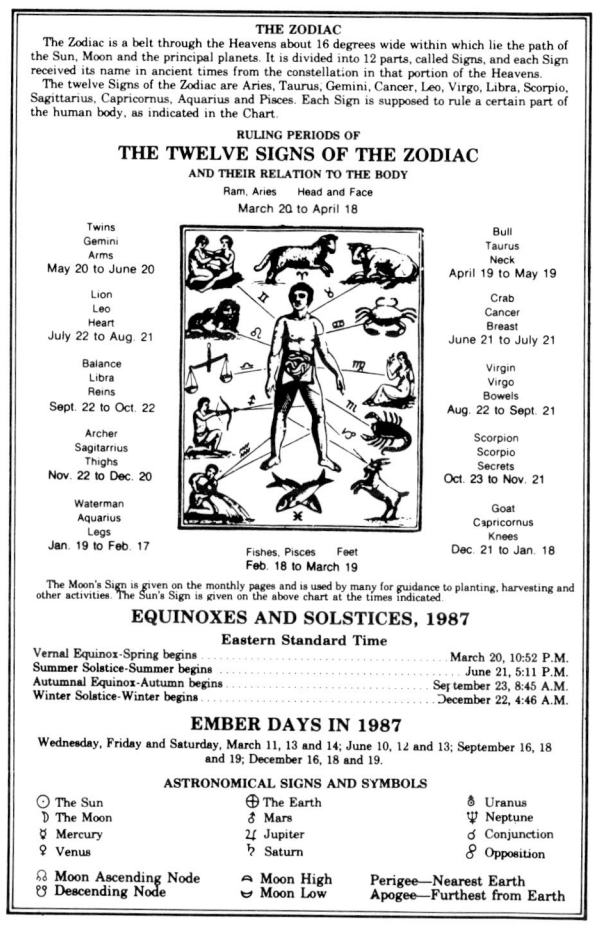

Used by permission of GRIER'S ALMANAC

Some canning was also done by the signs of the moon. Sauerkraut made on the New Moon would be crisp and white. It would also keep longer before spoiling. Jelly made on the New Moon produced more jelly for the amount of sugar put into the mixture, and it also boiled away less. Sweet potatoes should be dug and stored during the New Moon so they would not rot during the winter. It was also believed by some that root vegetables should be planted on dark nights, and that corn planted on dark nights would have fuller ears.

As with most things, every farmer in the early days, like every farmer today, prefers to believe that his ways of farming are the best. Farming today is far more scientific than just watching the signs, but some farmers take the best of both worlds to produce abundant crops each growing season.

Okra is one vegetable that seems to be a favorite for good summertime eating. The old-timey way to plant okra is as follows: After the ground has been laid off, drop the okra seed (plant thick) down the row. To cover the seed, walk over the row, stepping on the seed. This is usually enough dirt over the seed, as okra should never be planted deep. Planting should be around the first of April.

Suggestions other folks worked by:

* *Reset roses or root — New Moon in June.*
* *Never plant in the barren signs of Gemini, Leo and Virgo, as they are said to be only good for destroying weeds.*
* *Never dig potatoes when the moon is in the water signs of Cancer, Scorpio, and Pisces, as it is said, they will become moist and rot quickly.*
* *Harvest all root crops when the moon is growing old, as it is said, they will keep better and longer.*
* *Pick apples and pears on the full of the moon, as bruised spots will then dry up; but, if picked on the new of the moon, the spots will rot.*

Another forecast of rain was to watch the moon, and when one of its quarters had points turned downward, so that it would not hold water, it was going to rain on the earth. If the points turned upward, so that water would not spill out, there would be a dry spell.

Many of the mountain farmers would haul wagon loads of their vegetables to Gainesville, to sell to wholesalers there; or, they would hire someone to carry the vegetables to Atlanta to sell. Cleveland was approximately twenty-five miles north of Gainesville, and since there were no paved roads in the early 1900's, the trip usually took two days. There were wagon yards along the way, and the travelers would stop there to camp overnight. If there had been a rainy spell, the roads were sometimes so muddy, that the wagon bodies would be dragging the ground, and the horses would mire from six inches to a foot, while trying to pull the loaded wagon.

The number and breeds of animals found in the barn yard was usually one way of knowing whether or not a family was "fairly well off." For beef cattle, the Hereford breed was common. A good milk cow was a necessity. Some common breeds were the Guernsey, Jersey, and the Holstein. The cow had to be milked twice a day, and this chore was usually assigned to one of the children. The milk would be brought back to the house and strained through a cloth as it was poured from the milk bucket into a big mouth gallon jug. A piece of flour sack cloth was tied over the jug to keep it clean which was then taken to the nearby spring to keep it cool. If there was no running water on the farm, the milk jug might be placed in the well bucket and let down into the well, just above the water, to keep it cool.

When a cow was going to have a calf, she "went dry," meaning that she did not give any milk until she "came in" or "freshened," which meant that she gave birth to her calf. The cow's milk was not used by the family for about two weeks after the calf was born. For families who owned more than one cow, they just had less milk during this time; but, for those who had only one cow, they borrowed milk from a neighbor until their cow freshened. The milk was paid back when the neighbor's cow had a calf.

Buttermilk was something that every farm family enjoyed. It was good just to drink, or to eat with cornbread for supper. It was also used in cooking other great country treats such as biscuits, hoecakes, and flapjacks. It was made by pouring the sweet milk into a churn (usually made of clay) and allowed to sour. The milk was then churned with a wooden dasher, which had a paddle on the end which fit through a hole in the churn's wooden cover. As the dasher churned the milk, the butter was separated from the milk and rose to the top in a soft mass. When the milk had been churned enough, the butter was removed and placed into a bowl, where the remaining milk was worked out of it with a small, wooden paddle. The butter was then placed into molds to shape it and then removed onto a dish and stored in a cool place to become firm. The buttermilk, too, was placed here and stored in jars with tight-fitting lids or covered with a cloth.

Hubert Burke (Edna's dad) with one of his hogs and pigs which he raised on his farm in Habersham County.

Pork was one of the main staples of the family diet, and most families raised at least two or three hogs for slaughter each year. There were different breeds of hogs, with the more expensive being the Poland Chinas, Berkshires, and Red Hampshires. The Razorbacks were less expensive. Some farmers grew certain vegetables for the hogs, but usually they were given corn and fed the scraps from the kitchen. A bucket was kept in the kitchen or on the back porch for the scraps. It would be the responsibility of the children to "slop" the hogs everyday. This meant carrying the bucket of scraps to the "hog pen" and pouring the scraps or slop into their trough. The

Farming Was A Way Of Life

hogs also had to have water, and before running water came to the farm this meant drawing the water from the well or carrying it from the stream. Sometimes the hogs and cows were free to roam about a farm, but this was not the most common practice. Some farmers put a bell around the cow's neck, so if she did not come to the barn at milking time in the evening, she could be found more easily.

Another very important part of every farm were the roosters and hens. They not only provided fresh meat when needed, but the hens supplied the family with its eggs. Eggs were not only an important part of the diet then, but they were often the most in-demand and readily-available farm product used to barter with, when something was needed from the store. Also, the highlight of the week or month would come when a child could occasionally swap an egg for a stick of candy at the store! The chickens roamed the barnyard in search of food by day, and by night they roosted in the hen house, where they were always supposed to lay their eggs; except for the few times that it didn't work that way. When the eggs were going to be hatched, the mother hen would set on her nest and wait patiently for the baby chicks to hatch. There was nothing more enjoyable than  watching a mother hen and her baby chicks in the barnyard. There were several different breeds of chickens, such as the White and Black Leghorns, Rhode Island Reds, and Domineckers. When the preacher came, the family was almost always sure to have fried chicken for lunch, and more of everything else, too. The preacher was always fed the best the family had.

Superstitions were around then, as now. One strong belief was that if the rooster crowed during the night, something bad was going to happen. Crowing hens were also thought to be bad luck. When a mother heard her daughter whistling, the girl would be reprimanded with the following statement, "Whistling girls and crowing hens always come to some bad end."

Claude sitting on his mule that is hitched to his one-horse wagon. Circa 1955.

Fall was the time for the last work on the summer crops. It was the time to pull the fodder from the corn stalks. After the corn matured and was gathered, the leaves on the stalks began to turn brown and were ready to be pulled for fodder. It was used as food for the mules, horses, and cows. The fodder had to be pulled when it was damp, because when it was dry, the fodder was so brittle, it was difficult to gather and tie into bundles. The blades could also cut a person's hands if not handled with care. Because of the need to pull the fodder when it was damp, the family had to get up early and be in the field by daylight. This was necessary in order to get the work done before the sun dried the dew off the corn; then, they had to quit pulling the fodder until late afternoon. It was very common to pull 'way into the night to get the job done.

After the corn was gathered and in the crib, a lot of work was needed to shuck a crib full of corn an ear at a time. So, a way was found to work and have fun at the same time. The neighbors were invited over for a corn shucking. Every family tried to send at least one member, and sometimes entire families came. A game was played to see who could get the most points by finding red ears or red grains of corn. The host also provided a good meal for the workers. To feed such a large crowd, the food was usually cooked in dishpans. The corn shuckings were held at the houses of those neighbors who wanted help with their corn. It got the work done, and it provided a good opportunity to get together with friends and neighbors.

An old tradition of the mountains was that if a farmer had enough shucked corn to fill his crib then two neighbors would "tote" him into his house on a wooden rail (or a small tree). Claude's dad, Wiley Hood, was toted into his house when Claude was about 6 years old. That was the only time the family remembered seeing that done in their community. It was hard to fill the crib with shucked corn, and not many farmers were ever able to receive this old, traditional honor.

As the younger children grew up and could assume more responsibilities, the older boys would sometimes hire themselves out to work for someone who needed help on his farm and could afford to pay them. In most cases the arrangement was for room, board, and washing, plus maybe $10 or $15 per month. The boys lived as members of the family they were working for, until their job was completed. During the winter months, a job sawmilling brought in a few dollars for the farmer, if his boys were old enough to keep the farm running. Sometimes a man could get a dollar a day to cut and hew logs. The work ethic seemed to be different in earlier days. People did not know anything but hard work, but they were glad to work as long as it took to get a job done. One man relates his remembrances of his first job as a young boy. He was hired to chop cotton for 75 cents a day. He had to be in the field in the morning as soon as he could see and worked in the evening until he couldn't see. He said, "People didn't work by the hours then, they worked by the day; and whatever the person you worked for called a day, that was the day you put in. I was so glad to get that 75 cents, that I would have worked by flashlight for awhile!"

Life on the farms in the Georgia mountains may have been hard, but it was a good life. It was a time when the dignity, honor, and honesty of the person were more important than material wealth. The independent spirit of the pioneer was still strong, yet equally strong was the feeling in families, communities, and the individual that if someone was in need, and you could help them, you did, and you felt good about it. The communities were small, the families large, and there was great trust in their world.

Farming Was A Way Of Life

The Griffin Brothers Corn Mill in Clermont, GA in the early 1920's. John Griffin is on the left. (Georgia Department of Archives and History)

Griffin Brothers Cotton House in Clermont, GA during the early 1920's. John Griffin is in the foreground and Mood Griffin is pictured in the wagon loaded with hay. (Georgia Department of Archives and History)

Every Farm Had A Barn

Barns came in all sizes and shapes. Some were made of logs and others of boards, but they all served the same purpose. Barns were most important because they were used to house the livestock, store hay, grain, as well as farm equipment and supplies. Some were divided into individual compartments called stalls to be used by the livestock. There were cribs for corn, bins for grain, and lofts for hay.

As the farmer outgrew the original barn, he just kept adding onto it as he needed more space. Over the years, other farm buildings would be built around the barnyard to meet one need or another of the growing farm family. The farmer's barns and outbuildings were critical to the survival of his family. When a new barn was needed, or if an old one was destroyed by fire or storm, the neighbors would gather for a barn-raising to help build a new barn as quickly as possible.

Today many of the old barns have fallen into disrepair or have been torn down. They are frequently photographed and painted, but few are restored to their original beauty and usefulness.

Barns and Outbuildings

Barns and Outbuildings

Wiley Hood (left) walks around his barn in 1956. His farm was the most important thing in his life other than his family. Below are pictures of his barn and outbuildings years later.

Barns and Outbuildings

Barns and Outbuildings

Reading, Writing, and Ciphering

Restored Lydia School in Lumpkin County.

The community, one-room school was a place where the rural children could learn to read, write, and "cipher" (figure). The schools offered the children "booklearning." Grades one through seven were taught by the same teacher, in the same room. Often, several classes were taught at the same time, thanks to the help of the older, better students.

Most schools were usually built as near the center of the community as possible. In this way, all the children walked approximately an equal distance, which was between one and four miles. When a teacher lived and taught in different communities, daily commuting was not possible due to difficult traveling conditions. Often, a family living near the school would have a "spare" room, and they would invite the teacher to stay at their house during the school term.

Communities had great pride in their schools. Often, a property owner in the community would deed some land on which to build the school for as long as it was needed. After that time, the land would revert to the original owner or his family. Schools were built by each local community. There were no government regulations or financial assistance available to them. Each student had to pay tuition, which was not much, but families had very little money that could be spared for school. Books and supplies also had to be bought by the student. The few books that were needed were passed through a family from the oldest child down to the youngest.

A class of long ago at Lydia School. Notice Cedar Mountain in the background; also several of the children are barefoot. Someone's dog came to school for picture taking day.

In rural, North Georgia, during the 1800's and early 1900's, most students did not complete more than the first few grades, but a greater percentage of town children completed grammar and high school. This was due to the difference in the distance that a rural child had to travel and the different means by which town and rural families made their living.

Occasionally, a farm family was able to find one of its children a place in town to stay and a part-time job while continuing their education in high school. Upon arrival at school, however, the child might find that he was behind the students from town in his school work. Because their parents usually operated businesses, the town students' work and chore schedules did not require them to be absent from school as often as the students from rural areas. So if the farm child ever hoped to make a living by means other than farming, he had to have a lot of determination and work very hard.

Many little school houses once dotted the landscapes of the mountain communities. Some were one-or two-room schools. In White County, there were Pleasant Retreat, Mount Pleasant, and Blue Creek. New Bridge # 7 served that community in Hall County.

Hall County, GA 1904 - 1905. Students pose in front of New Bridge No. 7 located off U. S. Hwy. 129. This structure still stands and is used as a home by Charles B. Couch who is seen seated third from the left in the middle row. (Georgia Department of Archives and History.)

Reading, Writing, and Ciphering

A neglected Lydia School, before it was restored.

Lydia School was located in Lumpkin County. The first structure was built of logs, and the second burned. The third structure still stands today, representing a proud heritage. The school was built on land deeded by J. S. Jarrard, which was located on the east side of Porter Springs Road, some ten miles from Dahlonega, Georgia. Jarrard also deeded a six-foot wide, right-of-way for a path to a nearby spring. The beautiful location faced the majestic Cedar Mountain Camp Ground. No records exist of exactly how the school received its name. One story says it was named for the first woman who taught there, while another says it was named "Lydia," because it was the name of the Apostle Paul's first convert, when he preached in Macedonia (Acts 16:14).

The little school sometimes held as many as 60 students at one time, with classes being taught for grades one through seven in the one room building. The present school building was in use from 1915, until 1957. Then, the building fell into neglect and disrepair, though its memory remained strong in the mind of one of its former students. In fact, the appreciation and love of what the little school had meant to its students, for all those years, was very important to Loudean Jarrard Seabolt. It was her dad who had given the land to build the school. Her brothers and sisters had attended there, and many members of her family had taught at the school. Her first seven years of schooling were spent as a student at Lydia. After retiring from forty years of teaching in the White County School System, she set out to fulfill a dream. She wanted to bring Lydia School back to life, back to the original beauty she remembered from childhood. After much research, numerous treasure hunts for old items to replace those missing or damaged, and many more hours of hard work, her labor of love culminated in a beautifully restored and preserved piece of our history. Mrs. Seabolt uses the building for private functions and proudly shows it off to visitors and former students.

Loudean Seabolt poses in front of Cleveland Elementary School, 1950's.

Most parents wanted their children to learn to read, write, and "cipher". In short, they wanted them to get some "book learning." Then, as today, some parents were more dedicated to accomplishing this goal than were others. Some who wanted "schooling" for their children often just could not afford the loss of even one worker on the farm, and certainly not several school-age children who were the family's sole source of labor for making their livelihood. Other parents simply did not have the extra money for the books and supplies.

Farm children were given major responsibilities at very young ages, and they knew the importance of doing their share of the work on the farm. From the cradle, they learned survival first hand. They had very few choices in life. They did what they were told and did it the way they were told. The family unit was very important to the children at the time, because it was their only means of survival. This was the child's FIRST education in life. Those children, who were fortunate enough to go to school

Lydia School after restoration. By the front door there is a shelf for the water bucket and a gourd which was used as a dipper.

for one year, seven years, or beyond, were extremely proud of their accomplishments.

Children who attended school were up at daylight working to complete their chores before walking to school. Every day after school, they had to work in the fields, cut wood, shuck corn, or complete other chores which usually lasted until dark. Since there was little time for studying, the children had to make good use of the time available. Studying was often done before bedtime around the fireplace or on the eating table by the light of an oil lamp.

School terms were considerably different from the quarters and semesters of today's school year. School seemed more regimented and stricter, with the teachers having more control over the students. Cold weather often brought many hardships to farm children. They had to be outside in bad weather to care for the livestock and would sometimes get frostbite walking to school. One method used to keep the feet warm and dry was to wrap burlap bags around the shoes. These were then tied around the legs.

One reason children eventually dropped out of school was due to the fact that the older children in the family had more responsibilities on the farm. The older children had to miss days from school to help with such chores as the weekly wash, caring for the younger children, farming, etc. This also meant that the older teenager might be studying at a level with younger children. This sometimes was difficult on the ego and the patience. There were many factors that made the decision to quit school an acceptable one, and when it was done to help the family, it was often applauded as a very dutiful gesture. As the oldest left home, usually at 20 or 21 years of age, the same pattern was repeated with the next oldest child.

Most teachers kept a hickory (hickory switch) above the window or within handy reach, and they never hesitated to use it when there was a need. The switch could inflict a stinging welt to the legs of the receiver. A paddling board was also used. Some children knew that if they got a spanking or whipping at school, they would get another one when they got home. Somehow, this fact was a definite incentive to behave!

During recess and at lunch time the children played games. Most games had been learned from older children, parents, or were made up as they were played. In the early days, children could not go to the store and buy games and toys. The equipment for the games had to be homemade. Some of the games changed over the years, while others remained popular well into the mid 1900's, and are still played today.

The more popular games included:

Drop The Handkerchief

All the children stood in a circle facing inward for this game. The child who was "it" held a handkerchief and walked around the circle behind the other children. After selecting the next person to be "it," the handkerchief would be dropped quickly to the ground behind that person, hopefully without their seeing the handkerchief drop. Immediately, the child selected by the dropped handkerchief picked it up and ran after the person who was "it," trying to tag him before he could run around the entire group and return to the vacated place in the circle. If the one now holding the handkerchief could not tag the first person, they became the next "it" and repeated the process.

Red Rover

This was a game played by dividing the children into two groups or sides. Each side would stand in a long line holding hands tightly and then take turns calling a member of the other team to run toward their human chain. The person called over would try to break through their tight hold by running into them as hard as he or she could. After one team decided who to call over from the other side, they would sing, "Rover, Red Rover, send Bill right over." Bill would then charge toward the other team like a bull, and if he broke through the line, he went back to his team. If he failed to break the chain when he hit it he had to join the other team's side.

Go Fox Hunting

Children were divided into two groups — the fox team and the hunter team. Paper would be torn into pieces, and the fox team would drop the pieces of paper through the woods, leaving a trail. The hunter team would try to track and catch them. The fox team would try to be sly enough to mislead the hunters, including doubling back and catching the hunters. Sometimes, the children would go great distances into the woods playing this game.

Anti-Over

There were two teams, one on each side of the school house. One team member would throw the ball over the house, and when the other team caught it, the person making the catch would run around to the other side and tag as many members of the other team as possible. The winning team was the one that tagged all the members of the opposing team.

Marbles

In later years, marbles were popular for boys to play. The most fun was to have enough marbles to be able to swap and trade for what somebody else had. A person's favorite marble was usually his "shooter." It was also called a "taw," a "glassy," or a "monny."

Town Ball

This was a version of soft ball.

Board Games

Two of the more popular board games were dominoes and checkers.

Fox And Geese

The playing pieces were many kernels of corn painted red, with the remaining kernels being yellow or white. The red kernels (or yellow, if there was no red paint) were the fox, and the white ones were the geese (or chickens). The object was for the fox to catch the geese. This popular board game was similar to checkers.

For the most part, the boys and girls played separately. While the boys were playing games, most of the girls played house. In later years, it became more common for boys and girls to play together at school. As with the games played by children today, the games and rules mentioned previously had many variations, so adults today will often vigorously debate the "correct" terms that were used and the proper rules of play. The important point is that children of an earlier day learned at play how to get along with each other, how to compete as well as cooperate, and how to entertain themselves, each a valuable lesson in preparing for adulthood.

The class of 1937 at Lydia School with Ola Adams as teacher. Notice the girls holding their dolls.

There were no cafeterias or snack machines. Lunches were carried in lard or syrup buckets with lids. By the 1930's, some children used "dinner boxes." "Once in a blue moon" (once in a great while), a child might get to carry his lunch in a paper bag that had been used to bring something home from town. As the boys got older, they did not want to carry a lunch pail, so sometimes, mothers would wrap a biscuit and egg in waxpaper, and the boys would carry it in the hip pocket of their overalls. Many a biscuit was eaten that had been sat on for half a day. As it had been for years, the only drink available was sweet, mountain water from the spring or well.

A story is told of a family that was very poor, and the children of this family had only potatoes and some cornbread to carry for lunch. The other kids usually made fun of this, so most of the time the children would go off and eat lunch alone, so they would not be made fun of everyday. Then, after eating their lunch, they would go back and play. One day, a boy came to school with a little paper "sack" and yelled, "Who wants to swap lunches with me?" The little boy from the poor family was thrilled to death! He thought, "Now, I'll get some meat and biscuit." So, he said, "Me, me, I'll trade." And they traded lunches. The boy could hardly wait for lunch time to come. When the teacher rang the bell for lunch, he grabbed his little sack and headed out behind the school house. With great anticipation, he opened it, and there, instead of the meat and biscuit he had been craving and expecting, was a hammer and two hickory nuts! He had no lunch that day; but, he learned a lesson. He figured out right then and there that he was not the only poor kid in the county.

To get an education, our ancestors were required to make many sacrifices, but they did what had to be done and usually without question. Change and progress came slowly to the Georgia mountains, until the middle of the 20th century, and the educational system was no different.

Homemade Remedies

Medical care came slowly to the northeast Georgia mountains. Even after the time that a doctor was available in the area, many families could not afford to pay for a doctor's visit or any "store-bought" medicine. This lack of a professionally trained doctor, or a lack of money on the part of the folks who lived in the area, did not mean they didn't get sick and need medicine to help them get well. The mountain folks were accustomed to making do with what they had available; they were experts at the art of survival. They learned the roots, berries, trees, and other things around them, that possessed healing properties. Some of these remedies and cures came from the Indians. Over the years, more and more knowledge was accumulated and passed down orally from generation to generation.

There were usually one or two people in each community who were more knowledgable of sickness and the cures for each ailment. These people were called on whenever they were needed, and they always went to help their neighbors, never expecting pay. It was just what neighbors did. Despite these people's good efforts and best intentions, many of their remedies were no match for the diseases and epidemics which would sometimes strike an entire community. The sick were often brave souls, and their struggles to survive were noble, but all too often, they did not. They were accustomed to hard work from sunup to sundown. Most of the time they won enough battles to keep this constant struggle going, but when serious injury or dire disease struck, they were often completely helpless. Death was no stranger to the small communities. Even a minor injury could become a death call, as many times, there were no medicines, doctors, or hospitals close by, and there was little or no transportation in the early days.

Some of the old remedies were powerful medicines that worked as they were supposed to and would be healthy for today's generations. Other treatments would probably kill, if not from the actual results, just from the thought of what was being swallowed — for example, sheep manure tea! Sadly, few people today have a sufficient knowledge of the out-of-doors to gather the necessary ingredients to make the remedies. Also, some of the roots and plants no longer exist in the wild.

Some of the most dreaded diseases and illnesses in the earlier days were measles, typhoid fever, polio, mumps, whooping cough, tuberculosis, dysentery, and dropsy. A flu epidemic struck one community in White County, just after World War I. There were only two adult males in the community who did not have to be put to bed with the flu. This man and his son had to take care of all the chores for the entire community. They would go from house to house every day, getting wood for their fires, caring for their livestock, seeing to the food supply, and doing any other chores that were needed, while letting their own work go. They knew, without a doubt in their mind, that their neighbors would have done the same thing for them and their family. To keep from catching the flu, as they went from house to house, the two men wore a ball of asafetida (a bad smelling resin) around their necks, drank Red Pepper Tea (sweetened), and always ate onions before making their daily rounds. Whatever the reason, neither of the men "came down" with the flu during the epidemic.

In the mid-1800's, there were qualified physicians scattered throughout the area, and by the early 1900's still more came. Their offices were most often located in the largest town in the county, which was usually the county seat. Gainesville, the county seat of Hall County — being one of the most developed cities north of Atlanta — had more doctors than the outlying small towns in the surrounding counties. However, as always, transportation and money were problems for the rural county folks. In 1912, Dr. Henry Downey had the first hospital built in the northeast Georgia area. Located on South Sycamore Street, in Gainesville, it was called Downey Hospital. It is said to have probably been the first fully accredited hospital in the state. Dr. Downey came to Gainesville in 1901, to work for Pacolet Manufacturing Company as their company doctor at the New Holland Mill. Three years later, he moved his practice into Gainesville.

Downey Hospital was built in 1912, by Dr. James H. Downey. It was the only hospital in northeast Georgia for years. (Georgia Department of Archives and History.)

Cleveland, the county seat of White County, boasted up to three doctors and two dentists by the 1920's. Of these doctors, probably Dr. L. G. Neal was the most enduring, and therefore the best known in the area. Often he worked around the clock, seeing patients in his office and traveling throughout the hills to treat patients. He was a very loved and respected man in White County. He traveled by buggy in the early days, and when he was needed, someone had to ride a horse or walk to town to get him. Folks didn't have telephones then. Usually, he was only called if there was a serious need. It was a very common practice in those days to use a mid-wife to deliver babies, and there was a neighbor in nearly every community who birthed the babies. The use of the mid-wife declined in later years, and Dr. Neal began delivering more and more of the babies in the county. In many of the small communities, the records of the births and deaths in each family were kept by the most educated person in that community, usually the school teacher. Once each year, the teacher would make a trip to the courthouse to officially record the statistics of the community.

In the early days, using one's feet and legs was more important than it is today. There were no jobs on the farm for one who could not get around and very few jobs for a handicapped person in the towns or cities. To farm or to get from one place to another, a person had to be able to walk. Physical strength and endurance were key factors for the survival of an individual, especially if the father or mother became ill or handicapped. Polio was one of the most feared and dreaded diseases of the time, and it was no respecter of persons or ages in claiming its victims. If its victims survived the attack they were often left paralyzed. The severity of the disability varied, but it was permanent. Not until, 1955, did doctors find a means to control the disease.

Homemade Remedies

A minor, yet constant problem was "stumped" toes. All children went barefoot from Spring through Fall, and their toes always seemed to get in the way of something. Another problem was stepping on unseen objects which punctured the skin. This could sometimes become so serious that "blood poison" would "set-in," costing the person's life. The feet suffered still more abuse with the coming of winter months. Most work on a farm required folks to be outside. This included caring for the livestock, washing clothes, cutting and carrying wood, going to the outhouse, and walking three or four miles to and from school. All traveling done during the winter, whether it was in the wagon, on horseback, or walking, was done without any heat. A built-in heater was not one of the options offered when purchasing a new wagon! So, despite the best precautions they could devise, most people had to endure frostbite.

Frostbitten heels and toes were very painful. To help ease the pain, mothers would sometimes start a fire in a bucket and put pine tops on it. The feet were held over the bucket, and the heat and smoke from the pine helped ease the pain.

Since most illnesses were self-diagnosed, home remedies were the most available cures. If one remedy did not work, several others were tried, until one of them worked, or the patient just got well anyway in spite of the home remedy. There were a few store-bought items that most homes always kept on the shelf. One was kerosene. It was used to pour on injuries and mixed with other ingredients was often taken internally. Other medicines included: Black Draught, which was "good for whatever ailed you" — a cure all; Epsom Salts, for numerous disorders; baking soda, for burns and other things; and everyone's favorite, Castor Oil, which some say was measured out by the biggest spoon in the house and given to anyone who showed any sign of even thinking of being sick. It was common knowledge that the only correct way to take these and other "medicines," was to hold one's nose and swallow. Turpentine was another medicine which was good for a variety of ailments.

The following are some of the remedies used in earlier days:

Mumps: *Mostly were uncomfortable, but great care had to be taken not to work too soon and have a relapse or they might "fall." If this happened there could be serious complications, or even death.*

Whooping Cough: *Boil chestnut leaves in water, drain, and add honey. Drink for cough. Often when one member of a family "came down" with something, it was then passed on to others in the family. It was particularly disruptive when eight or ten kids in the same house coughed twenty-four hours a day with the whooping cough.*

Cough Syrup

1/2 cup honey	Combine all ingredients in boiler and cook over low heat until completely dissolved and syrupy. It is more effective when given warm. It used to be kept warm on the wood stove or heater, ready for use. Use at the first cough. (Mrs. Hubert C. Burke and Pearl Dixon)
1/2 - 3/4 cup brown sugar	
1/2 tsp. powered alum	
2 - 3 Tbs. vinegar	
1/3 stick butter or margarine	

Hives: *Red Alter Tea was used to break out the hives. The bark from the tree was used to make the tea. Care had to be taken to remove the bark correctly. To make the hives "come out," the bark should be scraped off with an upward motion. If the bark was scraped off with a downward motion, they would "go in." Also Catnip Tea would break out hives on babies.*

Measles: A serious illness, especially if they did not break out, and the patient's temperature was not lowered. The best remedy was Sheep Manure Tea. Recommended dosage for children was two tablespoons, four times a day. Yes, folks, it was just what it says — the ingredient for this one came from the barn! According to stories, many adults said they wouldn't drink the tea, but when they got sick enough, they decided the tea wouldn't be as bad as dying. Red Alter Tea was also used for measles.

Pneumonia: Mustard poultice was alternated with olive oil, to keep the skin from blistering.

Dysentery: Drink Blackberry Root Tea or drink the juice from the boiled berries.

Ulcers and Sore Mouth: Chew Yellow Root or make a tea and drink it.

Constipation: Drink Senna Leaf Tea.

Boils: Drink tea made from Red Alter for several days, and the boils will soon heal.

Nerves: Ginsing Root Tea.

Sore Throat: Slippery Elm Tea was good for this discomfort.

Sick Stomach: Drink Spearmint Tea.

Hypertension: Garlic was a sure cure.

Fever: Butterfly Root Tea was used to lower a fever.

Cough: Wild Cherry Bark Tea (sweetened); Rock Candy and whiskey; Horehound leaves, boiled, sweetened with syrup, and boiled down to a candy consistency.

Menstrual Cramp: Drink Wild Strawberry Tea; Ginger Tea and whiskey.

Nail Puncture: Make a poultice from peach tree leaves. Wash the wound with kerosene. Boil leaves until strength is out. Thicken the liquid with corn meal, and apply to the wound as hot as the body can stand.

Pneumonia: Boil hog hoofs in water and drink the liquid.

Ringworm: Mix turpentine and lard together, and put it on the ringworm. Also, boil walnut hulls in water, and rub the water on the infected area.

Rising: A piece of fat meat placed over the infected area would draw the rising to a head, so it would drain. Also, a slice of Irish potato placed on the infected area is said to draw the poison out.

Sting: One-half teaspoon of baking soda and one-half teaspoon of honey, were mixed together into a paste and put on the sting. Also, place tobacco or snuff on a cloth, add a few drops of water to moisten, and put it on the sting. This will take the swelling out.

Tuberculosis (also called "Consumption" and T.B.): Rabbit tobacco was pulled in the fields and dried. A pillow was then made, filled with the rabbit tobacco, and the person with "Consumption" slept on it.

Chest Congestion: Mix lard and turpentine together, put on a cloth, and place it on the chest. Or, beat mustard seeds to a powder and mix with a little flour and enough warm water to make a paste. Spread the paste over a cloth and place on the chest. It will begin to feel warm and may turn the skin red. The lard should keep it from blistering the skin. After using a poultice, the patient should be careful to remain dressed and/or covered well for awhile, as the pores of the skin have been opened, and it would be easy to catch fresh cold.

Colic: For babies, make Catnip Tea. It will help them to rest.

Picayunish: Picky. "You sure are being picayunish about eating your food today."

Plum: Totally (from: plumb). "We are plum out of coffee."

Pot Likker: Vegetable liquid. "After greens are cooked in water, the remaining liquid is called pot likker."

Purty Porely: Bad health. "Since his fall, Grandpa seems to be doing purty porely."

Quare: Peculiar (from: queer). "Everyone thought Grandma was a little quare, because she would never have a telephone put in her house."

Quietus: End. "Mama put a quietus on Bob's high living and late nights."

Reckon: Suppose. "I reckon it's alright for you to go home with Willie Mae."

Revenoors: Federal Revenue Agents. "The Revenoors were always snooping around in the woods near the mountain streams looking for moonshine stills."

Right Smart: A lot. "The children were sick a right smart last year."

Rostenears: Young corn (from: roasting ears). "Go down to the garden, and get you a mess of rostenears."

Step-Ins: Women's underwear. "Cora got six new pair of step-ins."

Switch (hickory): Small tree branch. "Mama often used a switch to spank Joe when he misbehaved."

Take On: To be emotional. "Jane sure did take on at Uncle Harold's funeral."

Tolable: Questionnable health (from: tolerable). "Yesterday, I was really sick; but today, I'm feeling tolable well."

Tote: Carry. "If we didn't take the wagon to church, sister would tote the baby for Mama."

Towsack: Burlap bag. "We put the potatoes in towsacks to take them to the cellar."

What In The Land: Expression preceeding a question. "What in the land have you got all over your new dress?"

Yarn: Story. "You never knew what to believe around Matthew, as he would tell one yarn after another, each one bigger than the last."

Other Words And Phrases Of The Time...

Bantam: A small variety of chicken. "Banty" was a term used to describe any small person with an aggressive personality.

Branch: A small stream or tributary of a larger creek or river.

Carry: To take, as to carry the butter to town.

Gap: Opening in a fence.

Gully Washer: A heavy rain.

Purt' Near: Almost.

Rattletrap: An old car that would barely run.

Sunday-Go-To-Meetin' Clothes: Best clothes that were worn only on Sunday.

To Saucer: To pour hot coffee from a cup into a saucer for the purpose of blowing it cool and slurping.

Took A Notion: Decided to.

Y'all: You all.

You'uns: All of y'all.

Younguns: Children.

Cooking Was A Tradition

Folks living in rural north Georgia in the early days depended entirely upon what they grew on their farms or were able to claim from Mother Nature in the fields and woods around them. The earliest pioneers of the mountain regions had to make their own fertilizers, preserve seeds from one planting season to another, and even sometimes borrow embers from a neighbor to start a fire with for cooking food or warming themselves. Providing food for themselves and their families was a daily challenge, and survival depended upon their ability to meet these challenges successfully.

Their success along with the changes that slowly came about over the years, gradually improved their way of life. Most families were able to provide an adequate amount of food for themselves in the early 1900's; there just was not a great amount of variety. An old phrase which says, "There's plenty, such as it is," was definitely true. Only during the Depression of the thirties and the rationing of goods during World War II was food limited for many mountain families, both in the amount and the variety.

In those early days there was no electricity, and thus, there were no refrigerators, electric stoves, microwaves, can openers, food processors, or lights. Trips to the store were infrequent, and even then, only the basics of sugar, salt, and coffee were bought. Everything else had to be made at home, and it took the entire family to get it all done. Every member of the large family had assigned chores. The cooking usually fell the lot of the women and the girls in the family; however, the boys often helped with the dishes and were responsible for seeing that there was a never-ending supply of wood for the cook stove.

The seasons played a prominent role in determining what would be seen on the table of hill folks at mealtimes. With spring came a special treat called "cress" (pronounced cre-sees). This was a small, green plant which grew wild, usually on creek banks and in the fields. The leaves, or "salet," were prepared as turnip or collard greens were — cooked with fatback, salt, and water. All these leafy greens were usually referred to as a "mess" of cress, salet, or turnip greens. Poke salet was another green enjoyed by some folks in the spring. It grew wild in the pastures and fields and was very plentiful. It had to be eaten when it was a young plant. The leaves were pulled off the stalk and cooked similarly to any other green. It was first parboiled (brought to a boil in water, then the water was drained off), fat back and salt were added, and then, it was cooked done.

As the early spring garden began to provide fresh vegetables, everyone's attitude began to improve. Fresh vegetables were a welcomed change from the winter fare. With the summer garden, the excitement then began to change, as basket after basket of vegetables and fruits were brought into the kitchen for preserving or canning for the next winter. Berries and fruits were the best part of summer. Blackberries, wild strawberries, huckleberries, scuppernongs, dewberries, apples, peaches, pears, and figs all made delicious pies, jellies, and jams. They were special treats just by themselves, too! As for the berries that grew wild in the woods, however, there was a price to be paid. The picker usually came home with briar scratches and chiggers in abundance.

Drying was a very common way of preserving fruits and some vegetables. They were prepared and spread on a piece of wood or cloth, then placed in the sun to dry, after which they were stored in bags or jars for use during the long winter months. Dried, green beans were called "leather breeches." Each bean pod was strung with a needle and thread, making a length of about two or three feet. The beans were then hung on the porch until they were dry. To prepare, they had to be soaked in water for several hours before cooking. They were cooked with a piece of fat back, salt, and water. Usually everything was cooked in black, iron pots and pans. They worked well on the wood stoves and fireplaces but were very heavy to lift.

Unless wheat was grown on the farm to make flour, the only bread the family had was cornbread. It was not uncommon to have cornbread for breakfast, dinner, and supper. Sometimes for supper, "mush" would be the main course. Mush was just cornmeal, salt, and water cooked until it had a good, mushy consistency. It was served in bowls with a glass of milk. Sometimes enough mush would be made to fry in hot grease for breakfast the next morning. It would "set-up" overnight, making it easy to slice and fry. Fried mush, syrup, and coffee made a good breakfast. Coffee beans were bought green at the store. They were parched in the oven at home, a few at a time, and every morning just enough were ground for the morning coffee. The coffee mill (grinder) was mounted on the kitchen wall. Very few families had coffee pots; the coffee was made in a boiler instead.

The fall of the year signaled the time to make cane syrup. The cane seed was planted like any other seed in the spring, and after it matured in the fall, the fodder was pulled for animal feed and the canes "stripped." The heads were cut off the stalk and the seed preserved for the next spring's planting. Then the canes were hauled to the syrup mill in the wagon. Unlike other mills which were powered by water, the syrup mill was powered by a mule. Through the syrup-making process, the juice was squeezed out of the canes and into a vat. The juice was then cooked into a syrup. Syrup was used as a sugar substitute when sugar was not available or affordable. Syrup bread, cookies, gingerbread, and popcorn balls were favorite foods made using syrup.

Another ritual of fall was that of slaughtering a hog to provide meat and lard for the family. The "hog killing" was not done until late fall, when the weather was cold enough that the meat would not spoil from the heat. Mother Nature provided the only refrigeration for the fresh meat. Many farmers believed in killing the hog when the moon was in a particular phase (killing the hog by the signs of the moon), while others had no faith in the signs. They killed when they thought it was cold enough, and when they had time and workers available. Pots of water were boiled, and the hog was usually shot and bled.

The hog was then removed to the prepared work area for dressing. The hot water was poured over the skin, so it could be scraped to remove all the hair. Then by the use of a pulley and rope, the hog was hung from a strong tree limb to be dressed. The internal organs were removed, and the hog was then taken to a table to be cut into hams, middlings, shoulders, and all the other parts of meat.

Since everyone had to kill their own hogs, usually the neighbors swapped out work with each other. After killing a hog, a "mess" of fresh meat was sent to each nearby neighbor. Everyone knew that they would get a "mess" in return when the neighbors killed their hogs. A delicacy enjoyed by many at hog killing time was the brains scrambled with eggs for breakfast or supper. Another delicious treat was tenderloin with cream gravy (thickened gravy) and biscuits. Scraps of meat, and any other portions the farmer desired to use, were ground up and seasoned with peppers, salt, sage, and other seasonings. This sausage was stored in corn shucks, or cloth bags, and then hung in the smoke house. In later years,

Cooking Was A Tradition

the sausage was fried to near done and canned in Mason jars. Still later, they were preserved by freezing. The smoke house was just that, a small, free-standing house, near the main house, where the meat was preserved, smoked, and stored. Actual open fires were kept burning in the house when meat was being smoked. There were also deep troughs or bins built of wood where some of the meat was packed in salt to be preserved. When a ham was to be cured, it was rubbed in a special recipe of spices and salt, placed in cloth bags, and hung in the smoke house to cure. The curing process usually took two to three months before the sugar-cured ham would be ready to eat.

Lard was very important to any cook of that time, so cooking the fat to render the lard was done with great care. There were two side benefits resulting from this. One was "cracklings," and the other was pork "skins." The lard was cooked in a large, usually black, iron pot over constant heat. Knowing just how hot to keep the fire was of great importance, as the lard would scorch easily. It had to be constantly stirred with a wooden stick. As the pieces of fat cooked to a crisp (crackling), they were removed from the grease. They were later chopped or ground up and mixed into the batter of cornbread. This corn "pone" was a welcomed change of taste during the winter months. The fire was removed from under the pot to allow the grease to cool. The lard had to be poured into churns or tin lard buckets before it got cold and became solid. When the lard was cooked at just the right temperature, it would be solid white. Lard made delicious biscuits and pie crusts. The skins could be cooked in the pot of lard, or cooked in the oven of the wood stove, until crisp. The skins were great for snacks, and since the farm children did not get snacks often, this was a treat. The hog's feet were properly prepared and pickled. Some children were allowed to make a balloon out of the hog's bladder; after it was washed and properly cleaned. The hog's intestines were also considered as being especially good to eat. They were called "chitlins" after they were cooked. They were washed, soaked for several days, and prepared using special recipes.

Recipes were family treasures passed from one generation to another. Wives and mothers took great pride in being considered the best cook in the community. All of the following recipes were contributed by family members and have been the basis of many a good meal. Also included here are ways of preparing certain foods which are not common to many of today's cooks. Here's to good eating!

Family Recipes

Apple Dumplings

6	baking apples (each about 3 inches in diameter), cored
	Pastry for two-crust pie
3	Tbs. chopped nuts
3	Tbs. raisins
1	cup water
2	cups brown sugar

Heat oven to 425 degrees. Prepare pastry as directed; roll into 14 inch square; cut into 4 squares and cut each of these in half. Place apple on each square. Mix raisins and nuts; fill each apple. Moisten corners of pastry squares; bring 2 opposite corners up and over apple and pinch. Repeat with remaining corners; pinch edges of pastry to seal. Place dumplings in ungreased oblong baking dish. Heat brown sugar and water to boiling; pour around dumplings. Bake, spooning syrup over dumplings 2 or 3 times, until crust is brown and apples are tender (approximately 45 minutes). Serve warm with cream.

Pastry

2/3	cup shortening or lard
2	cups all-purpose flour
1	tsp. salt
4 - 5	Tbs. cold water

Cut shortening into flour and salt until particles look like meal. Sprinkle water and toss with a fork. When all flour is moistened and pastry cleans side of bowl, roll out for dumplings.

Apple Butter

The following recipe is from an apple orchard, in 1928:

Cook apples in a small amount of water; mash up when done. For each cup of apples, add 1/2 cup sugar (add a small jar of apple jelly to 1 quart of apples). Bring to a boil, and cook until the mixture becomes thick. Add spices (clove, cinnamon and a little allspice). Scorches very easily and must be looked after very closely. Simmer for a long time to bring out the flavor.

Blackberry Jelly

Cook berries in enough water to cover. Remove seeds and measure the juice. Add two cups of juice to one cup of sugar. (About four cups of juice and two cups of sugar). Bring to a boil and cook hard for about 5 minutes. When it does not drop off of the spoon, it is done.

Old Fashion Butter Cookies

1	cup butter
3	eggs well beaten
2	cups sugar
1/2	tsp. salt
1/2	tsp. soda
1/2	tsp. vanilla
4	cups flour

Mix and roll very thin and cut with floured cutter. Bake on greased and floured cookie sheet. May be put in freezer or refrigerator and baked later.

Butterscotch Pie

2	cups light brown sugar
1	Tbs. butter
2	cups sweet milk
3	egg yolks
1/2	cup flour
1	tsp. vanilla

Mix and cook over low heat in heavy pan. Have pie crust baked. Pour filling into the baked crust. Pile meringue onto pie filling. Bake in slow oven.

Meringue

3	egg whites
4	Tbs. sugar
1/2	tsp. vanilla

Beat egg whites until stiff; add sugar and vanilla and beat until mixed.

Old Fashion Egg Pie

1/2	cup sugar
3	egg yolks
	dash nutmeg
2	Tbs. butter
1	cup sweet milk
2	tsp. flour

Mix and pour in raw pie shell* and bake. Use egg whites for topping. Beat and add 4 tablespoons sugar. When pie is almost done, top and allow to cook until brown. Cook at 250 degrees.

* Put the raw shell in the oven for a few minutes before adding the filling. This will keep the shell from coming to the top.

Family Recipes

Out Of This World Chocolate Cake
(Compliments of the Fox Hunter's Association)

First Step:

1 1/2 cups sugar
1/2 cup cooking oil
3 eggs
2 cups plain flour
1/2 cup butter
1 tsp. soda
1 cup buttermilk
1 tsp. vanilla
1 cup dates
1 cup chopped nuts

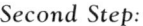

Second Step:

Blend sugar, oil, then the eggs one at a time. Add dry ingredients, milk and vanilla. Add dates and nuts last. Bake at 350 degrees for about 35 minutes. Use a large, square pan.

Third Step:

When cake is done, boil to a soft ball stage the following:

1 cup sugar
1/2 tsp. vanilla
1/2 tsp. soda
1 Tbs. Karo syrup
1/2 cup buttermilk
1/4 cup butter

Spread on cake; put back in the oven; cook for 10 minutes.

Fourth Step:

1 bar German chocolate
2 tsp. butter
1/4 cup water
1 1/2 cups powdered sugar and vanilla

Melt chocolate, butter, and mix with water. Cook over low heat. Mix in powdered sugar and vanilla. Put on cake.

Peaches For Fried Pies

2 gallons unpeeled peaches, cut-up
6 - 8 cups sugar
1 1/2 cups vinegar

Cook peaches, sugar, and vinegar until thick enough for pie filling. Can be frozen for later use.

Ginger Bread

1 cup shortening
1 cup sugar
1 cup molasses
4 eggs
2 tsp. soda
1 cup buttermilk
4 cups flour (plain)
1 tsp. (heaping) ground ginger
1 tsp. ground allspice
1/2 tsp. ground nutmeg

Cream shortening; add sugar, beating until light. Stir in molasses. Add eggs one at a time, beating well. Disolve soda in buttermilk. Combine flour and spices and add to creamed mixture with buttermilk. Cover and store in refrigerator until ready to bake. Batter can be kept up to 3 weeks. To bake, cook in a well-greased and floured iron skillet. Bake at 350 degrees until a pick comes out clean.

Peach Pickles

1/2 bushel peaches
5 pounds sugar
24 sticks clove

Peel peaches and wash. Put peaches in stone jar and cover with sugar. Sprinkle clove sticks over peaches. Let stand over night. Drain juice and bring it to a boil. Add peaches. Let heat through and put in can. Seal.

Pineapple Fritters

This is a 1935 recipe from a hotel in Clarkesville, Georgia.

1 can sliced pineapple (drained)
1 can milk
1 egg
1 cup flour

Mix well and beat until smooth. Dip pineapple and drop into hot fat (deep); allow to fry and brown. Remove one piece at a time and drain on paper. Serve with fried chicken. Serves eight.

Family Recipes

Pound Cake

1 lb. butter
1 lb. sugar
1 lb. eggs (8 large)
   vanilla flavoring
1 lb. flour

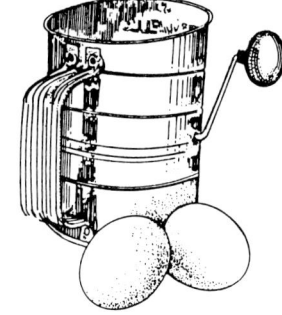

Cream butter, add sugar, and cream until fluffy. Add eggs and flour a little at a time. Beat well after each addition. Add vanilla. Bake in a tube pan lined with paper, greased and floured. Set stove at 275 degrees, and gradually raise the temperature to 350 degrees to brown cake. Bake for 1 1/2 hours. Frost if desired.

Frosting For Pound Cake

2 egg whites
1/2 cup water
2 1/2 cups sugar
1/2 cup Karo syrup

Beat egg whites in large mixer bowl. In an enamel pan, mix sugar, water, and syrup. Cook until mixture spins a thread. Pour half over beaten egg whites, beat a few seconds, then add remainder. Frost "Pound Cake."

Sweet Bread

2 cups molasses or cane syrup
1/2 cup butter
3 tsp. soda
1 1/2 tsp. salt
1/2 cup sugar
3 tsp. spice or ginger (optional)
3 cups flour

Heat molasses, add butter, soda, salt, sugar, and optional spice or flavoring. Work in flour. Roll out to round shape. Place in a greased, iron skillet. Bake at 400 degrees until tested with a broom straw, and it comes out clean.

Popcorn Balls

3/4 cup corn kernels
2 Tbs. Karo syrup
6 Tbs. molasses or cane syrup

Pop corn in popper with oil. While corn is popping, cook the syrup in a frying pan. When it begins to get thick or spins a thread, it is ready to pour over the corn. Mix to coat the corn. Grease hands with butter and make balls. Press lightly to hold together.

Tea Cakes

1 tsp. soda
3 cups flour
1 cup butter
1 cup sugar
1 egg
1 tsp. vanilla

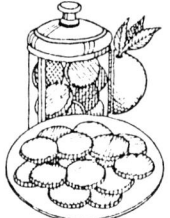

Sift the soda with the flour. Cream butter and sugar. Add beaten egg and flour. Roll out and bake.

In the early days, cookies were stored in dishpans and covered with towels, as there were no plastic or foil wraps.

Batter For Meats

(Recipe used by a Gainesville Restaurant, operating in the 1950's - 1970's)

6 eggs
1 can evaporated (large) milk
1/2 cup flour
   salt and pepper

Beat eggs; add milk and flour. Dip meat in mixture and roll in flour. Cook steaks 4 to 5 minutes; cook chicken 20 minutes. Cook in deep fat around 425 degrees.

Brunswick Stew

A recipe from a former County Agent of Habersham County — 1940.

12 lbs. beef
10 lbs. hog head or pork
2 lbs. pork liver
4 lbs. chicken
2 lbs. Irish potatoes
6 lbs. tomatoes
3 lbs. onions
3 lbs. broth
3 (14 oz.) bottles catsup
3 tsp. black pepper
2 Tbs. red pepper
   salt to taste
3 lbs. corn

Grind all meat after it has been cooked, mash potatoes after cooked in small amount of water. Cook tomatoes or use tomato juice. Add everything to tomatoes and simmer for a short time.

Family Recipes

Beef Tongue

Boil tongue until tender. Peel off the outer skin, and boil in salt water until very tender. Makes a great sandwich!

Cheese Biscuits

1/2	lb.	butter
1	tsp.	salt
1	lb.	grated cheese
1/4	tsp.	redpepper
4	cups	flour
2	tsp.	sugar

Blend ingredients and roll into log roll. Keep in refrigerator over night. Cut in thin wheels and bake. You get about 4 or 5 rolls. These may be frozen.

Chicken and Dumplings

Chicken:

2 - 3 pound chicken, stewed.

Remove chicken from broth and pull amount of meat desired from bones. Return chicken pieces to broth and bring to boil.

Dumplings:

3	Tbs.	shortening
1 1/2	cups	all-purpose flour
2	tsp.	baking powder
3/4	tsp.	salt
3/4	cup	milk

Cut shortening into flour. Add baking powder and salt until mixture resembles fine crumbs. Stir in milk. Drop dough by spoonfuls into hot meat and broth. Cook uncovered for 10 minutes. Cover and cook about 10 minutes longer.

Cornbread Dressing

3		eggs, boiled and chopped
1/2	cup	butter, melted
2	cups	cornbread, crumbled
1		onion, finely diced
2	cups	yeast bread crumbs
2	tsp.	sage
4	cups	broth
1/2	cup	celery (optional)

Combine all ingredients and mix well. Bake for 30 minutes at 350 degrees.

Chitlins

Clean the hog's intestines by running warm water through them. Split intestines open and wash thoroughly. Cut into pieces. Soak in salt water for several days, changing water every day. Boil in salt water until tender. Dip in a batter and fry until golden brown and crisp. Serve hot.

Cracklin' Cornbread

2	cups	self-rising corn meal
1		egg
1 1/2	cups	buttermilk
1	tsp.	salt
1 1/2	cups	cracklings, broken

Mix all ingredients thoroughly and pour into greased pan. (Put shortening in black skillet; add a little corn meal and allow to brown; pour in batter). Grease top of bread. Bake for 1 hour at 350 degrees.

Dill Pickles

Ingredients for one quart:

		white cucumbers
1/4	cup	coarse salt (1 can lid)
1/2	cup	vinegar (2 can lids)
2	Tbs.	dill seed per quart

Pack small, white cucumbers in quart jar and add salt, vinegar, and dill. Fill with cold water and seal. Shake the jar well to disolve the salt. Let set for six weeks before opening.

Hash

A 30 pound mixture — dated 1930.

3	lbs.	hamburger meat
1		hog head or pork
3		fryers
2	lbs.	onions
4	pts.	corn
5	lbs.	Irish potatoes (mashed)
4	Tbs.	black pepper
2	tsp.	red pepper
3	Tbs.	salt

Grind all meat together after it has been cooked. Grind onions and corn. Add the broth that the meat was cooked in and all other ingredients. Heat well and cool. Put in can.

Family Recipes

Pork Liver Mush

Cook 1/2 pork liver with salt and a small piece of fat meat. Remove meat and mash the liver. Put on stove and bring to a boil. Add red pepper and 1 teaspoon of ground sage. Add 1 cup corn meal with a little flour mixed in very slowly. If this is not enough to make real stiff, add more meal. Put in a pan to cool. Make into patties, roll in flour and fry. May be kept in refrigerator for days.

Syrup Taffy

2	cups sugar cane syrup
1	cup granulated sugar
3/4	cup water
1	Tbs. vinegar
4	Tbs. butter or margarine

In large sauce pan combine syrup, sugar and water. Slowly bring to hard-boil stage (260 degrees.), stirring during the latter part of cooking. Add vinegar; remove from heat and add butter or margarine. Pour into greased pan or heavy platter and when cool enough to handle pull until porus and light in color. Do not squeeze. Stretch into long rope, twist and cut into pieces. Wrap in waxed paper.

Sugar-Cured Ham

(Ingredients and steps to follow in preparing a fresh ham for curing)

For Each Ham:

2	cups salt
2	Tbs. black pepper
1	pt. brown sugar
2	Tbs. red pepper
1	Tbs. saltpeter

Mix all ingredients together and rub the ham while it is warm. Wrap in brown paper, and hang up with hock down to drain. Put in a cloth bag to hang. Do not open for two months.

White Mountain Icing

1	cup sugar
1/4	cup white corn syrup
2	Tbs. water
2	egg whites
1	tsp. vanilla

Cook sugar, water and syrup rapidly to 242 degrees. Beat egg whites until stiff enough to hold a peak. Pour hot syrup rapid-rapidly over egg whites. Continue beating until it stands in a stiff peak, add vanilla. Spread icing over cake layers. (This icing is especially good when sprinkled with coconut.)

Baptist And Methodist Influences

Many of the early settlers who came to America did so to escape religious persecution. However, some of these settlers of the New England colonies found continued harrassment for worshiping as their beliefs dictated. Among certain of the colonists there was a gradual southward movement in search of more freedom of worship.

The Baptist Denomination

The Baptist denomination of today developed primarily from the Puritan churches that had been established during the Reformation which began in 1517, and from the Anglican Church. A group of believers separated themselves from the Anglican Church and became known as Separatists, and later as Baptists. In 1620, the Pilgrims being a Separatist group led by William Brewster, established the Plymouth Colony. Roger Williams founded a Baptist church in Providence in the Rhode Island Colony in 1639. Over the next three centuries the Baptist denomination grew and spread, and by the early 1900's it was the largest Protestant denomination in the United States.

The Baptists are perhaps the most diverse groups of any denomination in America. There are scores of groups who use the name Baptist in one form or another, but their beliefs and practices are not always the same. Most groups do believe that a person must voluntarily accept Christ as Savior, and choose to become a member of the Church. Each individual congregation has complete autonomy within the denomination. There is no hierarchy which controls churches. Although there is the organizational structure of the Southern Baptist Convention and the Georgia Baptist Convention, their position and decisions are not binding on member churches. The Bible serves as the source of authority on matters of faith and doctrine. Often there have been more differences than points of agreement causing groups to divide and form a new church supporting their particular beliefs. This considerable variety of philosophies endorsed by the Baptist ranges from liberal to very conservative, and even then there can be differences within groups from church to church. Not every Southern Baptist Church or every Primitive Baptist Church may share the same doctrines.

A new Baptist church can be constituted whenever and wherever a group of worshipers meet together desiring to form a church which will teach their beliefs. To state their exact beliefs, the group or church membership writes their Abstracts or Articles of Faith and presents them to the membership for approval by a majority vote, and they are considered adopted as the official statement of what that church believes. Rules of Decorum are also written and adopted. These rules state the manner in which all conferences or business meetings of the church are to be conducted. The Church Covenant is also adopted. Although similar in each church, they are usually different in some details.

The following Church Covenant, Articles of Faith, and Rules of Decorum were taken from the original 1929 Church record book of Mt. View Baptist Church.

Church Covenant

Adopted September 1929-

We trust we have been brought by Divine Grace to embrace the Lord Jesus Christ, and by the Influence of His Spirit to give ourselves up to Him. So we do now Solemnly Covenant with each other, That God enableing us, we will walk together in Brotherly Love; That we will exercise a Christain Care and Watchfulness over each other, and faithfully warn, rebuke, and Admonish one Another, as the case may require; That we will not forsake the assembleing of ourselves together, nor Omit the great duty of Prayer, both for ourselves and for others; That we will participate in each other's Joys and endeavor with tenderness and Sympathy to bear each others burdens and Sorrows; That we will endeavor to bring up those under our care in the nurture and admonition Lord; That we will Seek divine aid to enable us to walk circumspectly and watchfully in the world; denouncing all Ungodliness and worldly lust; That we will Strive together for the Support of a Gospel Ministry Among us; That we will endeavor by example and effort to win Souls to Christ; and through life, amidst all reports, Seek to live to the Glory of God who hath called us out of darkness into his marvellous Light.

Abstract of Faith
Adopted September , 1929

1- We believe in one only true and living GOD; The Father, Son and Holy Ghost – Three in one –

2- We believe the Scriptures of the Old and New Testament are the word of God, and the only rule of Faith and practice.

3- We believe in the Doctrine of original Sin –

4- We believe in Man's inability to recover himself from the fallen State that he is in by Nature, by his own free will and Holiness –

5- We believe in the Doctrine of Election according to the Scriptures, through Sanctification of the Spirit and belief of the Truth –

6- We believe that Sinners are justified in the sight of God only by Faith in Our Lord Jesus Christ –

7- We believe that Saints shall persevere in Grace and not finally Fall away –

8- We believe that Baptism and the Lord's Supper are Ordinances of the Gospel, and that True Believers are the only Subjects of Baptism, and that "Immersion" alone is Baptism, And that Believers are the only proper Communicants of The Lord's Supper –

9- We believe in the Resurrection of the Dead and in a General Judgment –

10- We believe that the Joys of the Righteous and the Punishment of the Wicked will be Eternal –

11- We believe that no MAN has a right to the Administration of the Ordinances, except such as have been called of GOD, and regularly Baptized, and approved of by the Churches, and come under Imposition of Hands by a "Presbytery"

Rules of Decorum

Rule 1st. All Conferences shall be opened by Singing or Prayer.

" 2nd. The Church shall have a Moderator and Clerk who shall be elected by the Church.

" 3rd. Call for fellowship.

" 4th. Invite visiting Brethren to Seats.

" 5th. Opened the Door of the Church.

6th The Clerk shall minute each Meeting In a Book kept for that purpose and shall be read at next Meeting.

7th Each member have a Right to speak in all cases, who shall arise to his feet and address the Moderator.

8th. No Member shall speak more than Three times on the same subject without leave of the Church.

9th. No Member shall absent themself in time of Conference without leaf of the Moderator.

10th. The Moderator may speak in all cases provided the chair be filled.

11th Every Motion made and Seconded Shall be brought before The Church, unless withdrawn by the mover —

12th A Majority shall rule in all cases. Except touching fellowship, and that shall be Unanimous —

13th The Moderator shall not vote unless the House be tied, then has the right to cast the deciding Vote —

14th If two Members arise at the Same time the Moderator Shall decide who Shall speak first —

15th The Moderator Shall be deemed a Judge of Order and Shall call to its observance at any time —

16th Private or Personal Offenses will be carried out According to The 18th Chapter of Mathew —

17th Amendments To These may be made at any time, by a Majority of the Church while in Conference — if they deem it necessary —

18th Call for General Business —

As late as the 1940's, it was common for rural churches to have worship service only on one Sunday of each month. Conference was held only once each month, usually on the Saturday before preaching on the following Sunday. Later, Sabbath School (Sunday School) was held every Sunday. Then more churches became "half-time" instead of "quarter-time" churches, meaning they had preaching on two Sunday's each month. Today some rural churches remain on this schedule, but the majority of all churches are now "full-time" having preaching every Sunday of the month.

Strict rules of moral behavior were set forth by earlier churches, and the membership was expected to follow those rules. It was not uncommon for the rules to state how many conferences a male member could miss before he would receive disciplinary action. One rule often read that the Moderator call for peace and fellowship of the members. If it was a husband and wife, two neighbors, or whomever, the minutes recorded that "all were not found in peace," and a committee would go to the homes of the squabblers to discuss the matter with them. Usually they had to come to church at the next conference service and confess their wrong. After hearing the evidence, the congregation would vote to forgive the offenders. For more severe offences such as drinking, dancing (playing), adultry, and others, the member could be "turned out" of the church (excommunicated). To some extent, churches of earlier years passed and enforced the laws by which members of each small, rural community lived. The elders of the churches became the judge with the membership acting as the jury. For the most part this was accepted by members of the community. Most communities were fairly isolated, and although every family was very independent, they all knew each other and about each other. There were very few rules and regulations from outside sources such as government agencies and the multitudes of other regulations which we have today; therefore, their lives were simpler. Most folks lived during the week what they heard on Sunday, and the Golden Rule was their way of life.

The officers of the Baptist church were the minister and the deacons. Each Baptist church congregation elected their own minister and deacons. The deacons, having met the criteria given in I Timothy 3: 8-13, were chosen by the church membership. The deacon being a member of the church or a layperson within the church assisted the pastor in worship services, assisted with Communion (one of the ordinances of the church symbolizing the Lord's Supper or Jesus' Last Supper before he was crucified), and assisted other church members with any physical or spiritual needs. They oversaw the finances of the church and represented the church in the community as they saw a need. Today, the officers of the Baptist church continue to be elected by the individual memberships. However, in churches having larger congregations the pastor now has other officers to assist him in addition to the deacons.

Differences within the Baptist denomination of years ago were not so dissimilar to the issues which cause discord and animosity among church members today. Heated discussions were often created by such issues as falling from grace - whether once saved, always saved; belief in missions and educational programs - whether they should be supported by organized efforts of the churches; church ordinances - whether there are two or three to be observed; and predestination - whether or not what will be, will be. Additionally there are differences in styles of music, a formal order of worship for services, programs and activities available within each church, and others. Prior to joining any denomination or church one should be knowledgeable of its doctrines and agree with its practices.

Southern Baptist
The largest number of Baptist churches in the south are those associated with the Southern Baptist Convention. The Southern Baptist Convention was organized in Augusta, Georgia, during a meeting held May 8-12, 1845. At that time there were already signs of sectionalism and controversy over the

slavery issue between the Southern Baptist and the Northern Baptist (now the American Baptist). After the War Between the States the two Baptist groups did not reunite, and Southern Baptist churches grew and expanded across the South and Southwest.

The Southern Baptist Convention developed a strong central organization, yet allowed the individual church to maintain local autonomy. Rather than having a hierarchy at the top, it developed its strength from the bottom up. When the Convention met it was made up of "messengers" elected by local churches to represent their various opinions and beliefs. Each of these messengers had a say in policies developed and recommended to the churches as a whole. The SBC was especially effective with its work in missions, home and foreign. They have always been evangelistic and dedicated to spreading the gospel around the world. Today there are thirty-seven state conventions belonging to the Southern Baptist Convention. The number of churches exceed 37,000 representing an individual membership of 14,616,781.

On the state level the Baptist in Georgia met at a much earlier date to organize themselves into associations. These were groups of churches who met to share ideas and problems and to give mutual help and support one to the other. The first association to be formed was the Georgia Association, in 1784, with two associations soon following, the Hephzibah and the Sarepta. They met twice each year in the beginning and annually, later. Growth and cooperation continued among the Baptist throughout the state.

On June 29, 1822, the Baptist Convention of the State of Georgia, was organized at Powelton Baptist Church, in Hancock County. Earlier, in 1801, 1802, and 1803, meetings had been held at Powelton Church to discuss the continuation of organized work by Georgia Baptist. However, there was still no clearcut direction for the denomination as a whole to follow in order to accomplish joint goals in areas of missions and cooperative work with other denominations. These meetings laid the foundation for the Georgia Baptist Convention. The name first used by the body was "The General Baptist Association of the State of Georgia." The first moderator was Jesse Mercer. He was an active leader in the establishment of the Convention as well as Mercer Institute in 1833. Named for the Reverend Mercer, the Institute later became Mercer University. The Georgia Baptist Convention was the second state Baptist convention organized; the South Carolina Convention had been first in 1821.

With the formation of the Convention, Georgia Baptists were not only able to focus more attention on mission work but also on Christian education. The establishment not only of Mercer Institute, but many other schools and academies throughout the state, were witness to the Convention's commitment to become more heavily involved in education. Following the Civil War a greater interest in benevolent ministries emerged. As a result of caring for many of the children who were orphaned because of the War, the Georgia Baptist Children's Home came into being. The Georgia Baptist Hospital (Georgia Baptist Medical Center), and homes for older adults were additional facilities created later to provide care to those individuals needing their services. There are today, ninety-two local associations across the state making up the Georgia Baptist Convention. These associations currently represent some 3,041 Baptist churches, having a total membership of 1,186,995. These churches are served by 2,709 Pastors.

An association is made up of churches in a given region for fellowship, cooperation, and mission work. Each association has a slate of officers elected at the annual meeting which usually lasts for two days. This annual associational meeting is held at different churches each year. Delegates are elected by each church to attend the meetings and represent their church in any business matters which might be presented for discussion and a vote. Reports are submitted by each church showing their financial contributions to the Convention's various programs, as well as the number of baptisms, additions to the church by transfer of letter, the enrollment of special programs within the church such as Sunday School, Training Union, Vacation Bible School, Brotherhood, and others. In order to belong to a local association a church must make application for membership. After examination, if they are found to be orthodox in Baptist doctrine and principle, they are accepted into the association. Any church that becomes unacceptable in faith or practice may be dropped from the association's membership. Also, any church may withdraw itself from the association when it chooses.

As needs have changed over the years, so have the associations. Some of the first mountain associations have reorganized, changed names, or just disbanded. More than one association often served the same area, thus the church membership had a choice of which one to join. One of the oldest associations in the northeast Georgia mountains is the Chattahoochee Baptist Association. It was organized in 1826, at Hopewell Baptist Church in Hall County. The county was only eight years old at that time. The Association began with only nine churches and today has grown to over fifty member churches.

Claude Hood has worked with many associations during his ministry in five north Georgia counties. He served as Moderator of the White County Baptist Association for eleven years, 1957-1968 and worked with the Chattahoochee, Chestatee, Enon, Habersham, and Liberty Associations.

During his years of ministry, Claude has always been careful to respect everyone's right to their beliefs and way of worship. He has never hesitated to state what his beliefs are, and why he believes as he does, yet, he believes every individual has freedom of choice. He has never based a friendship, or the decision to work with another minister or lay group, upon their interpretation of every verse of the Bible as long as there is agreement upon its basic principles as God's inspired Word.

The following is a statement by the Chattahoochee Baptist Association as their Declaration of Faith. It expresses the basic beliefs of the Southern Baptists. However, within this group of Baptist, as with most other groups, there are degrees of conservatism, liberalism, and those who seem to remain in the middle of the debates.

Declaration of Faith

We, the Baptist churches of Christ who have been regularly baptized on a profession of faith, are convinced by a series of experiences of the necessity for a combination of churches and of maintaining a correspondence for the purpose of preserving a federal union among churches of the same faith and order, and as we are convinced that there are a number of Baptist churches who differ from us in faith and practice, and that it is impossible to have communion where there is no union, therefore, we think it our duty to set forth briefly and concisely a declaration of the faith and order upon which we are constituted.

FIRST, *we believe in one only true and living God, the Father, Son and Holy Ghost, Three in One.*
SECOND, *we believe the Scriptures of the Old and New Testaments are the words of God and the only rules of faith and practice.*
THIRD, *we believe in the doctrine of original sin.*
FOURTH, *we believe in man's inability to recover himself from the fallen state he is in by nature, by his own free will and holiness.*
FIFTH, *we believe in the doctrine of election according to the Scriptures.*
SIXTH, *we believe that sinners are justified in the sight of God only by faith in our Lord Jesus Christ.*
SEVENTH, *we believe the saints shall persevere in grace and not finally fall away.*
EIGHTH, *we believe that baptism and the Lord's Supper are ordinances of the Gospel, and that true believers are the only subjects of baptism, and that immersion is the mode, and that baptized believers are the only proper communicants.*
NINTH, *we believe in the resurrection of the dead and a general judgement.*
TENTH, *we believe that the joys of the righteous and the punishment of the wicked will be eternal.*

ELEVENTH, we believe that no minister has a right to the administration of the ordinances, only such as have been called by God, regularly baptized, approved of by the churches, and come under imposition of hands by the presbytery.

Southern Baptists observe two ordinances of the church: baptism and the Lord's Supper. It is their belief that Jesus gave definite commands concerning the observance of baptism and the Lord's Supper, and that He gave no command concerning footwashing.

Primitive Baptist

Primitive Baptists believe Jesus commanded that three ordinances be observed: baptism, the Lord's Supper, and footwashing. In Georgia, these and other differences in Biblical interpretation and matters of belief began to surface in the 1830's, and came to final action in 1840, when the group known as the "Anti-missionary" Baptists separated themselves from the Georgia Baptist Convention. As missions, education, and benevolent services found more organized support within the Baptist group affiliated with the Convention, those opposed came to be called "Primitive" or "Hard-Shell" Baptists. Many of this group also believed in "predestination." Before this movement reached Georgia, it had been readily accepted on the frontier and was especially popular in the Ohio Valley region.

Independent Baptist

Independent Baptists share some similar beliefs with the Southern Baptists, with the Independents being more "fundamentalist." They are strong in their beliefs about evangelism, personal witnessing, the virgin birth, the death, burial, and resurrection of Jesus, and His second coming. Their ministers deliver a message of hell and damnation or heaven for eternity. The most important command to the church is the salvation of the "lost." Worship services of the independent churches are usually more informal and do not have a prearranged order of worship to follow. Usually in favor of missions, they prefer direct support, allowing the individual church to have control of their funds, thus money is not wasted on organizational costs. There are no official denominational affiliations. Independent Baptists are enthusiastic and are often led by strong charismatic pastors.

Free Will Baptist

Free Will Baptist gets its name from its most important belief, that of the individual's free will to choose. Like other Baptists, they believe the individual has free will to choose Christ, but unlike other groups, they believe at some future time the individual is equally free to reject Him. This argument has long been called "falling from grace." Other groups within the Baptist denomination believe "once saved, always saved." Their analogy is that a person cannot be physically "unborn," thus it is not possible to be spiritually "unsaved" once saved.

The Free Will Movement began in the 1700's, but was not nationally organized until 1935. They were later known as the National Association of Free Will Baptists, with offices located in Nashville, Tennessee. They support missions, believe in the three ordinances: immersion baptism, the Lord's Supper, and footwashing. There will continue to be debates over the major difference in the doctrine of the Free Will Baptists of "falling from grace" and the other Baptist groups who preach "eternal security" and "preservation of the saints."

* * * * *

This discussion has touched briefly on but a few of the groups calling themselves "Baptist." They are such an independent group, that in reality, it could be said that each church does something different from every other Baptist church, thus allowing the local congregation the independence and opportunity to define and attempt to meet its own needs and those of the community it serves.

The Methodist Church

The Methodist Church played an important role in the life of a developing nation. Methodists trace their beginnings back to John Wesley, a Church of England clergyman in the 1700's. Methodist churches are evangelical, stress salvation through faith, and emphasize a Christian life and God's forgiveness of sins. It is their belief that each individual must declare his faith in Jesus Christ publicly. The Bible is their guide in religious matters. Baptism in the Methodist church is not by immersion, but by the minister dipping his fingers in a font of water and placing them on the head of the individual or sprinkling the water over the individual's head. Many Methodists are baptized into the church as babies, rather than church membership being a decision of choice later in life.

John Wesley visited America only once. In 1736, he traveled to the new colony of Georgia; however, he soon returned to England, where he preached that salvation was free to all men, not just to a select few, and that God's grace was equal to every need. By the late 1700's several lay (unordained) preachers had been sent to America to preach the gospel. The Methodist Church set about to carry the gospel to the frontier, and by the mid-nineteenth century they had become the largest Protestant denomination in America. The Circuit Riders were a large reason for this success. They were able to preach to the most isolated communities and establish churches wherever they went.

Not only were the writings of John Wesley important to the Methodist Church, but Charles Wesley is equally remembered for the thousands of beautiful hymns he wrote, which are enjoyed today by all denominations and faiths.

During the early part of the twentieth century most every church in north Georgia was either Baptist or Methodist, and some church buildings were used by one denomination one Sunday and the other the next. Some even shared their Sunday School Superintendents. One year the Methodists would elect the Superintendent, and the next year the Baptists would elect. There was great cooperation between the two groups. They all lived in the same community and were neighbors and friends. Although most of the campmeetings were Methodist, they were equally attended by the Baptists.

There is a hierarchy of the Methodist leadership. There are three basic ministerial offices of the Methodist Church: deacon, elder, and bishop. The bishop holds the highest office. The national legislative body is the General Conference which meets every four years. At the Annual Conferences of each local region ministers are ordained and receive appointments to the churches which they will pastor.

Although the Methodists did not divide as often as the Baptists, they have had some differences over the years which have caused divisions within the church. The first organized Methodist Church was called the Methodist Episcopal Church. From this group the Methodist Protestant Church, the Methodist Episcopal Church, and the Methodist Episcopal Church, South evolved, to reunite in 1939, as the Methodist Church. In 1968, the Methodist Episcopal Church was joined with the Evangelical United Brethren to form the United Methodist Church, and today is the largest Methodist body in the United States. However, over a dozen other groups also use the name Methodist. The

Mossy Creek United Methodist Church in White County, was established in 1821. The first building was of hewn logs. In 1947 the present building was constructed.

Baptist And Methodist Influences

Congregational Methodist Church, the Wesleyan Methodist Church of America, the Free Methodist Church of North America and numerous other groups comprise the list of Methodists.

Not only has Claude had many friends who were Methodist, his mother was reared in a Methodist family and attended Mossy Creek Methodist Church during her childhood. During the early years of Claude's ministry in rural north Georgia the Methodists and Baptists helped each other when there was a need, cooperated, and shared in each other's joys and sorrows.

Dinner-On-The-Ground

In earlier days of community church life when there was to be a morning and an afternoon service, folks would prepare lunch for their families along with a little extra for sharing. With transportation being by wagon, neither time nor comfort allowed them to go home for lunch and be back at church in time for the afternoon service. There was also the matter of catching-up on all the latest community gossip and news during lunch. For young people, it was a great time for "sparking."

Claude second from right, late 1940's.

Quilts or table cloths were spread on the ground, and the food was then "set-out." Later, tables were built in church yards and greatly improved the enjoyment of the all-day functions. Everyone prepared the best dishes they could afford. Folks went from quilt, or from table to table, sampling everyone's food. It was quite an honor to be known as the best cook in the community.

In more recent years shelters have been placed over the tables, improving the odds greatly of not being driven inside the church to spread lunch on benches or getting wet because of a sudden summer storm. Today, most rural churches have a fellowship building where meals are served in a climate controlled setting with no ants, flies, or inclement weather. Without question this is a wonderful improvement and convenience. Nonetheless, it seems a little sad that the children growing up today will never fully appreciate the art of balancing a plate piled high with food and a cup of tea, while you fight with flies, sweat bees, and all the other insects which have singled out the food on your plate as their lunch. It may still be called "Dinner-on-the-Ground," but it "ain't" the same!

Singing Schools

Singing Schools were common in earlier years. They were usually two weeks of teaching, learning, fun, and rejoicing in song. Old and young alike met at church every evening during the two week period and learned to read and sing by "shaped-notes." The notes were called do-re-mi-fa-sol-la-ti-do with each note having a particular shape and sound. One could learn to read music by shaped-notes or by lines and spaces. Shaped-note music was usually taught and sung in rural churches of the South. This style of singing was sometimes called "Sacred Harp Singing," "Convention Singing", or "Harmony Singing." The singing school often closed with an "All-Day-Singing" and "Dinner-On-The-Ground." Folks would come from miles around to enjoy these singings and good country cooking!

The Early Years

The Early Family History of Claude Edward Hood

Claude Edward Hood is the third of nine children (seven boys and two girls) born to John Wiley and Mollie Elizabeth Allison Hood. Born on December 19, 1909, in White County, Georgia, Claude has lived most of his life there. During his late teens he lived in Canton, Ohio where he worked in a steel mill, returning home to the family farm to help his dad at the age of twenty. He was the first child to leave home. This loss impacted the family emotionally and physically. Although Wiley had several younger children to help with the farm work, the return of Claude to the farm was a great benefit, because as an adult, he was able to put in a longer, harder day's work. At this time Claude's youngest brother was only five years old, so his parents were still very busy rearing children.

During the early years of their married life Wiley and Mollie rented farmland and a two-room log cabin in the Town Creek area of White County. The family lived in the cabin until Claude was nine years old. Five of the Hood children were born while the family lived there. The family attended church at Hood's Chapel. Although interdenominational, it was mostly made up of Baptists and Methodists. Years earlier, before the children's time, it had served as the community school. As a young boy Wiley attended school at Hood's Chapel. Occasionally, Wiley would invite the preachers from the Chapel to stay overnight with them. When they came, the children would have to sleep on the floor so the preachers could have their bed. Around 1918, Wiley bought a farm having approximately one hundred seventy-five acres. The farm was located in the same community, only a few miles from their cabin.

Claude started school at the age of five, but like most farm children living in rural North Georgia then, farm work came first, and this caused him to get behind in school. Claude and all his brothers and sisters went to Pleasant Retreat School, located in the Town Creek Community (later, part of the community was called Mt. View). Mae, the oldest sister, married Jessie Black, who as teacher at Pleasant Retreat, taught most of the Hood Children. Claude quit school at 17, when he completed the sixth grade. However, after a few years in the ministry, Claude felt the need to continue his education. He attended Clarkesville High School for a short time, but later enrolled at Cleveland High School where he graduated in 1938, with 46 other students. His was the largest graduating class, to date, in the history of the school.

Cleveland High School, Class of 1938.

Claude Hood

Graduating Class of 1938. Claude is second from the right on the front row.

The Class poses in their Sunday best. Claude on back row, third from the right.

The Early Years

Cleveland High School
Cleveland, Georgia

Some of the students of Cleveland High in 1938. Claude is pictured at bottom left.

* * * * *

Cleveland High 1938 Class Roll

Willela Allison, Charles Barrett, Eula Black, Lucille Black, Neal Black, Dillard Blackwell, Lucille Brady, O. Y. Cook, Jr., Joe Davidson, Marcell Dorsey, Margaret Dorsey, Vernon Dorsey, Louise Glover, Carl Gunter, Sarah Gunter, Claude Hood, Louise Head, Harriett Hunt, Henrietta Hunt, William Johnson, Hampton Keith, Ray Keith, Robert Kenimer, Charles Lawson, George McCollum, Georgia McCollum, C. J. Meaders, Vergie Meaders, L. G. Neal, Jr., Ellena Nix, Jack Nix, J. L. Nix, Nola Mae Palmer, Wallace Palmour, Ernestine Reynolds, James Reynolds, Estelle Rich, Thelma Scott, Ray Skelton, Paul Smith, Tom Staton, Beulah Mae Stovall, Franklin Thomas, Edith Thurmond, Lillie Mae Wheeler, Fred White, and Ruth White.

Class Colors: Blue and White   *Class Flower: Red Rose*

The public school system then was comprised of only eleven grades. In 1947, the Georgia General Assembly passed legislation to establish twelve grades, but it was a few years before funding was available to implement the plan. Claude entered school in the seventh grade at the age of 25, and in order to complete the required work as quickly as possible, he carried extra courses whenever possible. Additionally, he continued as pastor of several churches and farmed to support himself and to help his dad. Despite Claude's age difference with his classmates, he formed many friendships during those years that are still an important part of his life. Claude went on to attend Truett McConnell College and completed numerous courses at Mercer University and the University of Georgia.

Claude lived at his parents' home until he was 34. The early years of his ministry were the growing-up years of his younger brothers and sisters, and they all became involved with his ministry to some degree. Occasionally on Sundays his many friends and church members would come home with Claude after he had delivered the Sunday morning message. They would have lunch with the family and enjoy the afternoon singing or sitting on the front porch talking and being with friends.

Claude standing on the front porch of his homeplace with his parents.

The brothers and sisters always looked forward to company, because it meant that they would be treated to their mother's best cooking which she reserved for company. Sometimes during revivals company would spend an entire week with the Hood family.

All was not fun, however, as Claude's younger sister recalls having to iron Claude's shirts. She ironed as many as fourteen at one time so he would have enough to last during the weeks of revivals. Material then was not wrinkle free; they had to be ironed damp, with a heavy cast iron that was heated in the coals or on the wood stove. Because he was away so much of the time, Claude often received help in plowing his crops from some of his brothers and his dad, when they could spare the time away from their own crops. He also hired folks to help him with the crops sometimes.

The Hood family usually worked more than from sunup to sundown. One sister remembered Claude sitting at the kitchen table studying his Bible by the light of a kerosene lamp until 2 o'clock in the morning. After Claude's work in the ministry began, his mother always gathered the children around at bedtime and read the Bible to them. She usually asked Claude to pray the evening prayer, but when she led the prayer she always prayed one particular phrase which each child still remembers today. She closed each of her prayers by praying, "God bless my dear children."

Both the Hood and the Allison families seemed to have been blessed with an abundance of ministers who have served numerous Baptist and Methodist churches. On Wiley's side of the family there were three cousins, Rev. Jim Hood of Union County, Rev. R. W. Allison, and Rev. Charlie Ledford, and one uncle, Rev. Jim West who were Baptist ministers. Rev. J. Herman Allison of Atlanta, Mollie's brother, pastored many Methodist churches throughout Atlanta during his ministry. Rev. John Franklin and Bishop Marvin Franklin are her cousins. Her mother's sister, Eliza Franklin, was the grandmother of Dr. Charles Allen, formerly of Atlanta and presently living in Texas. His mother and Mollie's cousin Lula Franklin Allen was the wife of Rev. Bob Allen. Her cousin Pearl Franklin married Rev. Ben Smith. While reared in the Methodist faith, Mollie joined the Baptist church after her marriage to Wiley. She and Wiley were members of Mt. View Baptist Church, where they are buried.

The Hood/Allison Families

Ed and Rosa Hood

Mood and Matilda Allison

As Time Passes...
Wiley and Mollie Hood

Wedding Picture, 1906

During the 1940's

Fiftieth Wedding Anniversary, 1956

The John Wiley Hood Family

A family portrait in 1925, (front row, l-r) Tom, Wiley, Lillie, Mollie, and Jim; (back row, l-r) John, Lester, Mae, Claude, and Fred Hood.

Wiley and Mollie Hood sit in front of their home in 1910. Fred is the child standing, and Claude is the baby in his mother's lap.

Claude and Fred at home in 1930

Hood/Allison

Posing in the snow for a traveling photographer in 1929, (front row, l-r) Tom and Jim; (middle row, l-r) Lillie, John, Lester and Fred; (back row, l-r) Mae and Claude.

The family in the 1950's (front row, l-r) Claude, Fred, Wiley and Mollie; (back row, l-r) John, Tom, Lester, Jim, and Mae (Lillie was absent).

Hood/Allison

The Wiley Hood family in 1953 (front row, l-r) Wanslie, Mary and Irene Hood, Jesse, Jr., and Ray Black, Leon, Claudette, Clyde, Edna, and Vernon Hood; (middle row, l-r) Jim, Tom, John, Claude, James, Tommy, Mary Frances, and Charlotte Hood; (back row, l-r) Betty, Jesse, Sr., and Mae Black, Myrtice Hood, Wiley Black, Lester, Wiley, and Mollie Hood, Leroy Black, Lounette and Fred Hood.

Wiley and Mollie stand in front of their house.

Celebrating fifty years of marriage, Wiley and Mollie pose with (front row, l-r) Fred, Mae and Claude; (back row, l-r) Jim, Lester and Tom.

Hood/Allison

The Anniversary Celebration held in the back yard of the homeplace, overlooking the Hood farm. On the distant hill is the house Wiley had built for Claude and Edna in 1944.

Wiley's sister, (l-r) Pearl Warwick, and his brother Claude G. Hood; Mollie's sister, Nettie Autry and her brother Lester Allison, circa 1956.

Pictured at Fred's Fiftieth Wedding Anniversary, (l-r) Lester Hood, Mae Black, Lillie Turner, Claude, Fred, and John Hood, (Tom absent).

Early Family History Of Edna Burke Hood

Edna was the youngest of four children of Hubert and Lola Dixon Burke. She was born July 14, 1923, in Habersham County and spent most of her growing-up years on the family farm located just outside Clarkesville, Georgia, on the Cleveland Highway. Beaver Creek ran through the Burke property and the Soquee River bordered the family's land. Hubert owned sawmills, farmed, and raised hogs, cattle, and sheep. He was a generous man and enjoyed helping others whenever he was able to do so; whether it was giving lumber to build new churches, hay and a truck for a hayride, watermelons for a watermelon cutting, or giving help to a neighbor needing his expertise as a country veterinarian. Several hired hands lived and worked on the Burke farm, while others worked at the sawmill. Edna's mother usually kept food cooking on two stoves in order to provide three meals each day for her family and many of the hired hands. For several years Edna helped her dad by keeping his company's books.

There was always an open door to relatives, friends, and neighbors. Relatives often came for extended visits, and folks always dropped by to share Lola's good cooking. Hubert was a very strong-willed man and usually his word was "law" to his family and those who worked for him. He was not afraid to fight for what he believed. Although he had to work hard all his life to provide for himself and his family, he also believed in having a good time. He enjoyed hunting, camping, fishing, or just going for drives on Sunday afternoons. His family was usually included in these outings. Work, like fun, was frequently shared with relatives living nearby.

Because their farm was so close to Clarkesville, Edna and her family felt equally a part of daily town life as well as farm life. After graduation from Clarkesville High School in 1940, Edna went to work for an attorney and was paid $5.00 a week. She later worked for Stovall's Dime Store where her pay was raised to $7.00 a week. As a result of World War II there were more government jobs available, and in 1943 Edna went to work for the Federal Government with the War Price and Rationing Board.

During the War such things as tires, kerosene, gasoline, bicycles, and certain food items were rationed. To buy goods which were on the government's rationing list one had to have, not only the money, but also government-issued stamps to accompany the money. Sales were not supposed to be made without the stamps. Store owners had to account for, and show a balance between, their sales, stamps received, and remaining stock.

The War Ration Books were numbered and dated and contained sheets of small coupons which were also numbered. The book had to be officially stamped and signed by the user when issued. If an individual, for example, ran a business using trucks and needed more gasoline or tires than a normal stamp book would accommodate, it was necessary to go to the Rationing Board office and make application for those items. After consideration, the local Board would then rule on the application. If approved, a special certificate was issued. These certificates along with the ration stamp books had to be kept locked in a vault because of their value. If not, they would be stolen and sold on the black market, which often presented additional problems for government officials.

INSTRUCTIONS

1. This book is valuable. Do not lose it.

2. Each stamp authorizes you to purchase rationed goods in the quantities and at the times designated by the Office of Price Administration. Without the stamps you will be unable to purchase those goods.

3. Detailed instructions concerning the use of the book and the stamps will be issued. Watch for those instructions so that you will know how to use your book and stamps. Your Local War Price and Rationing Board can give you full information.

4. Do not throw this book away when all of the stamps have been used, or when the time for their use has expired. You may be required to present this book when you apply for subsequent books.

Rationing is a vital part of your country's war effort. Any attempt to violate the rules is an effort to deny someone his share and will create hardship and help the enemy.

This book is your Government's assurance of your right to buy your fair share of certain goods made scarce by war. Price ceilings have also been established for your protection. Dealers must post these prices conspicuously. Don't pay more.

Give your whole support to rationing and thereby conserve our vital goods. Be guided by the rule:

"*If you don't need it*, DON'T BUY IT."

16—32299-1   ☆   U. S. GOVERNMENT PRINTING OFFICE : 1943

War Rationing Book issued in 1943, to Robert N. Howell at Tournapull, Georgia, in Stephens County.

UNITED STATES OF AMERICA
OFFICE OF PRICE ADMINISTRATION

N⁰ 593449 BL

WAR RATION BOOK No. 3

Void if altered

NOT VALID WITHOUT STAMP

Identification of person to whom issued: PRINT IN FULL

Robert _N._ _Howell_
(First name) (Middle name) (Last name)

Street number or rural route _P.O. Box 12_

City or post office _Tournapull_   State _Georgia_

AGE	SEX	WEIGHT	HEIGHT	OCCUPATION
2 yr.	Male	32 Lbs.	Ft. 3 5 In.	

SIGNATURE _Robert Newton Howell_
(Person to whom book is issued. If such person is unable to sign because of age or incapacity, another may sign in his behalf.)

WARNING
This book is the property of the United States Government. It is unlawful to sell it to any other person, or to use it or permit anyone else to use it, except to obtain rationed goods in accordance with regulations of the Office of Price Administration. Any person who finds a lost War Ration Book must return it to the War Price and Rationing Board which issued it. Persons who violate rationing regulations are subject to $10,000 fine or imprisonment, or both.

OPA Form No. R-130

LOCAL BOARD ACTION

Issued by _____
(Local board number)   (Date)

Street address _____

City _____   State _____

(Signature of issuing officer)

The Early Years
101

Clarkesville High School, Class of 1940

Edna Burke Hood graduated from Clarkesville High School in 1940, at which time there were still only eleven grades. There were 51 students in the Senior Class. The group went to Washington, D. C., for their class trip. Edna is the eleventh from the left on the front row.

On September 2, 1944, at the age of 21, Edna married Claude E. Hood of Cleveland, Georgia. By this time Claude's ministry was well established, and by 1945 he was pastoring five quarter-time churches, one full-time church, and had numerous other obligations. These churches were spread over three counties and required a considerable amount of traveling throughout the church communities. In addition to his regularly scheduled commitments, Claude was kept busy responding to requests for help from people throughout the counties where he served in meeting a multitude of needs.

His concern and interest took many forms, some of which were providing transportation for medical needs, counseling, speaking to judges and other public officials on behalf of someone in trouble with the law, working with adoption agencies, the Red Cross and branches of service about hardship cases, and much more. Payment for his services was given mostly in the form of love, friendship, and respect, since most folks living in rural northeast Georgia at this time did not have jobs which generated extra money to pay for help of any kind.

Edna soon learned that Claude's dedication to his calling took precedence over their home life. Being constantly on the go left her with little time to do the things she enjoyed such as cooking, sewing, working in her home, or visiting her family. However, she quickly adjusted to her new role and to the demands placed on her as a minister's wife. Her warmth and kindness, combined with her youthful beauty and genuine concern for the people she met, helped her win acceptance wherever she went. Edna put her many talents to work right away directing Vacation Bible Schools, Christmas Pageants, and working with young people in other areas of the churches. While at home, she was equally as talented in her ability to make a house into a home.

Edna has never taken her responsibilities lightly, and today she continues to do the many things that ministers' wives must do, such as assuring that Claude has the necessary and appropriate clothes to stand before a congregation, that he meets all of his appointments, and assisting Claude with all the other demands which are made on him and his time. Although semi-retired, Claude and Edna still maintain a busy schedule.

As their years together have passed, Edna has always enjoyed the accolades given to Claude when everything was running smoothly; yet, she has also felt the pain and known the sorrow which ministers often feel when working with people. She has seen the physical and emotional fatigue and the great physical pain sometimes endured because Claude was more concerned about the needs of others than his own. Edna has been by his side through a life-threatening case of mumps and double pneumonia, back surgery which left him unable to walk for several weeks and unable to resume his normal work pace for several months, and a serious automobile accident with full recovery taking over a year. In 1986 Claude was told that he had cancer. Nevertheless, because of Edna's constant encouragement and support, Claude's strong will to keep on going, and many prayers offered in his behalf, he has thus far been able to continue with his work although at a little slower pace some days.

Through forty-three years of marriage, Edna has stood by Claude when he could not stand alone, supported him when he needed a hand, encouraged him when he was down, and delighted in the good times while working in their home and in their churches. But most of all, as his constant companion for so many years, Edna has been, and continues to be, Claude's best friend and the love of his life.

The Taylor Lafette Burk Family
(spelling later changed to Burke)
(Hubert Coleman Burke, Edna's father, was the son of Taylor Lafette Burk.)

Hubert Burke (second from left), poses with his parents, Taylor and Lillie, and other brothers and sisters. Circa 1905.

The William Sherman Dixon Family
(Lola Belle Dixon Burke, Edna's mother, was the daughter of William Sherman Dixon.)

Pictured are (back row, l-r): William and Louvada Dixon, Cora Lee, Lessie, Pearl, and Carrie; (front row, l-r) Marlor, Lasco, Carl, Bertha Mae, Arvil, and Lola Bell; (inset, l-r) Garlin and Ellis. Original photograph was made in 1910 - inset was added several years later.

The Hubert Coleman Burke Family

Hubert during the 1940's.

Hubert in his stylish work clothes.

Lola at her home near Clarkesville, Georgia.

Burke/Dixon

Hubert C. Burke, early 1900's.

Pictured are (front row) Hubert and Lola Burke; (back row, l-r) Frank, Coleman, Cora Lee and Edna Burke in 1925.

The Burke children in 1928, (l-r) Frank, Cora Lee, Edna, and Coleman. The boys are wearing knee-knockers (pants) and are barefoot.

A cold winter at Dr. Hardman's farm in Habersham County; (l-r) Eleanor McConnell, Cora Lee, Edna, and Coleman.

Burke/Dixon

Frank Burke.

Coleman Burke.

Edna Burke.

Cora Lee Burke.

Edna (left) and Cora Lee Burke.

Burke/Dixon

Hubert and Lola in front of Claude and Edna's house, 1950's.

The Hubert C. Burke family. Pictured at the homeplace in Clarkesville are (back row, l-r) Ervin Wilson, Claude Hood, Frank, Coleman, and Frances Burke; (second row, l-r) Edna B. Hood, Cora Lee B. Wilson, Debbie Burke, Norma Burke; (third row, l-r) Claudette H. Howell, Lola Burke, Ann Wilson; (front row, l-r) Craig (Claudette's son), Teresa, and David Burke. Circa 1971.

In the early 1960's, pictured are (l-r) Lola Burke, Edna B. Hood, Cora Lee B. Wilson, Coleman, Frank, and Hubert Burke.

Memories And Shadows Of Another Time
...Gone Forever.

Hubert and Lola shared many good times during their years together on this homeplace. Here they reared their children and their grandchildren came to visit. Here too, each remained until their death.

The William (Will) Sherman Dixon Family

The Dixon children, (l-r) Arvil, Carl, Bertha, and baby Garlin, early 1900's.

At a Dixon Family Reunion in the 1950's are (l-r) Ellis Dixon, Garland Dixon, Bertha D. Hill, Carl Dixon, Arvil Dixon, Lola D. Burke, Lasco Dixon, Carrie D. Sosebee, Pearl Dixon, and Lessie D. Berry.

Dixon Family Reunion in the 1960's. Dixon brothers, sisters and in-laws.

During the 19th century and well into the 20th, there were very few major life choices available to folks in North Georgia and not a great number of minor choices. Since the opportunities to achieve, acquire, and change were indeed limited, what little was acquired and achieved usually took longer, and the personal cost was greater. Despite everyone's hard work, they were barely able to make a living from farming. At the time most folks had little, or wanted little, because there was less to want in rural areas. Jobs and ways to earn money were few to none. Having most things in common with their neighbors, the majority of people were content with their lot in life. B. Aldon Dixon, in the "Dixon Family History," tells of the difficulties encountered by a man and his family as they struggled to survive on a small farm in Habersham County, and the challenges they later faced as "mill-hands" working in the Habersham Cotton Mill. The story was not unique to the Dixon family. Rather it tells of the hardships that confronted most families during those years.

William Sherman and Louvada Pruitt Dixon

"William Sherman married Louvada Pruitt on Christmas Day, 1888, and within the year they had the first of their twelve children. They lived in the north end of Habersham county in Nachoochee Valley. The young couple lived next door to Will's parents until the fall of 1906. A severe hail storm completely destroyed the crops that year, and because they had nine children at the time, they were forced to leave Nachoochee and move to Habersham so they could provide for their large family. Will became an oiler in the carding room of the textile plant. This move was to change the course of the family's history from an agrarian life to that of a poor cotton mill "hand." Will continued to work there until his death in 1923. As the children reached 12 or 14 years of age, they dropped out of school to begin work at the mill in order to aid in the support of the family. The family never owned an automobile. They raised hogs and cows at their rented Habersham Mills home."

The Dixon Reunion at Fairfield Baptist Church, in Habersham County, 1950's. This Fairfield Church building has since burned and been replaced with a new brick structure.

The Ministerial Years

After seventy-eight years of traveling through the foothills of northeast Georgia, fifty-five of which have been spent delivering a message of love, hope, and salvation, Claude Hood is still carrying this same message to congregations today. It was in the summer of 1931, at the age of 22, that Claude knew his calling in life was to become a minister, to help his fellowman and to deliver God's message to those who would hear it. However, almost immediately after this realization, he began to have doubts and thoughts about all of the reasons why he should not make a public announcement of his decision, therefore avoiding a total commitment. He reasoned that he had not studied the Bible very much, had not completed his education, certainly was not a public speaker, knew little of the rules and decorum of a church, and most of all, although he liked and respected preachers, he had never wanted to become one. He fought with these doubts for almost nine months before determining that he would announce his decision to become a minister after the summer revival at Mt. View Baptist Church. However, as often happens in life, the best made plans sometimes are changed. Instead of waiting until after the revival, Claude told of his decision during the revival, and with that announcement in 1932, he made a public commitment of service to God and his fellowman — a commitment which he has honored since that day.

Claude and Edna at Pleasant Grove Baptist Church, in the late 1970's.

Rev. Homer Thomas, the pastor of Mt. View Church, invited Claude to preach his first sermon that week and to assist him with revivals at five churches during that summer. The first revival was at Yonah School which served as a mission under the sponsorship of the First Baptist Church in Cleveland. (Years later the church of Mt. Yonah was constituted on June 22, 1958, with twenty-two charter members.) From Mt. Yonah they went on to Center Grove, Friendship, Town Creek, and Tesnatee Baptist Churches for one week of revival services at each church. At that time, in the early thirties, most folks in the area still walked or rode in wagons to church; only a very few people owned an automobile.

Claude in 1932, his first year in the ministry.

Claude was young, inexperienced and often fought feelings of inadequacy that summer when he would stand to deliver his sermons to seasoned ministers of the Gospel and to members of the church who knew the Bible from cover to cover. Rev. Thomas scheduled Claude to speak every other day at the morning and evening services. Revivals were the highlight of the summer for the local communities, and both Christians and non-Christians usually attended the services. A dual purpose was served by the revival, in that it was a time for spiritual renewal as well as the social event of the year in the rural areas. Most farm work was put aside for a week, and old acquaintances and friendships were renewed. Often, churches were filled to capacity and usually overflowed into the yard, as folks from neighboring communities came to attend the revival services.

Summer revivals were especially enjoyed by the young people. It was a great time for courting because there were so many more boys and girls at church during the revival. At that time, a church function was the best place to find a sweetheart. Being the middle of summer, the churches were very hot. There was additional heat from the oil lamps which were used for light. One might get a small amount of relief from a hand-held fan, which was usually donated by the local funeral home. Even after there were electric lights in the churches, it would be years before electric fans or air conditioning became commonplace in rural churches.

Although all windows were raised on those hot summer nights, there was little chance of feeling a breeze. When the church was filled to capacity, men and boys usually sat on the window ledges, thus blocking any flow of air that might come into the building. During the summer revivals Claude's clothes would often be completely wet with perspiration when he finished delivering his sermon. He would sometimes take along a light weight overcoat to wear out into the night air. Then, as in later years, consecutive weeks of preaching day and night, followed by weekends back at the churches he pastored, left him completely exhausted. Claude recalls being so physically tired that sometimes he was not sure whether he could care for his livestock and crops after weeks of preaching; but just when he thought he could not continue, his strength was always renewed.

During the early years of Claude's ministry, preachers were often invited to stay overnight in the homes of church members. It was a long-standing tradition in most communities to welcome the preacher into one's home. The best food the family could prepare was cooked when the preacher came. The first summer Claude helped in revivals was a new experience for him. It was physically draining, and he was usually ready for a good night's sleep when the opportunity came. On one particular night, early in their association, Claude and Homer were very tired when they went to bed. Homer "slept like a log" (very soundly); but, Claude tossed and turned all night. The next morning, Homer asked him if he slept well, and Claude allowed that he did not rest well at all. Something kept biting him, but he did not know what it was. After dressing, the two men went to the back porch to wash-up before breakfast, where their host greeted them and asked if they had slept good. Homer said, "I did, but Claude said something like to have eaten him up last night! He didn't get any sleep." To which the man replied, "Well, I guess it was bedbugs, we've got 'em." Homer later expressed regret that he had mentioned the problem to the man. He just did not think of bedbugs because they did not bother him, but Claude was definitely bothered by them. That night was his first, but not to be his last encounter with bedbugs. Sometimes his clothes would have numerous blood stains on them from their bites. Despite all of his close encounters with bedbugs over the years, Claude never carried them home on his clothes.

During the last week of revivals that first summer, Claude began to show symptoms of something other than fatigue. He had been exposed to the measles, and never having had them, his body seemed to be thinking that it was the right time to experience them. When he got home that weekend, he was very sick and continued to get worse until the measles finally broke out. All his family, with the exception of his dad, caught them from him. His younger sister and mother were seriously ill during their bout with the measles. It took the family three weeks to completely recover and return to their normal schedules.

While interviewing friends and acquaintances to gain information and historical data for the writing of this book, the following observations and thoughts were expressed about Claude during his earlier ministry and his impact on the area. Also noted was the duration of his influence on people in predominantly rural areas in the counties where he has lived and worked. Some of these people have known Claude since he was a young man, while others have become acquainted with him only in more recent years.

"There were lots of preachers then, but most were older than Claude. At every revival, they wanted to get Claude to help. Having to go day and night all summer to revival was hard work. I wondered sometimes how he held out. There was no money for the preachers; folks didn't have the money to give much. Claude was the kind of person who was so sincere in what he said. When he got up to preach, they listened to him. If anything is ever mentioned about him, he's one of the finest men that ever lived. All that bunch (around one particular church in White County) felt that way about him. Everybody young and old loved Claude - still do!"

"I remember his first sermon at our church. I thought he was great! He was so young and interested in us and sincere in what he was doing. We were used to older men at that time. We were really blessed when he came to run a revival. The young really caught his enthusiasm, but both the old and young followed him. There were no generation gaps then. There was full fellowship."

"I was in my early teens when Claude came to pastor our church. I remember that he seemed so polished, his dress was always very neat and stylish. He had a car and visited everybody in the community, and that hadn't been done before. His leadership was different from anything I'd ever heard or seen before. He was able to capture the imagination of the whole community and bring it together. It seemed that some preachers thought you couldn't worship unless there was a lot of emotionalism at every service, but when Claude preached, people responded to the basic preaching of the truth of the Bible more than emotionalism. He didn't try to force anyone to accept Christ; he didn't embarrass anyone by pointing them out. Claude preached his sermon, gave the invitation, and respected the individual's right to make a decision about Christ and the Church. He just let folks know that he was concerned about them, loved them, and that God loved them. Everybody knew that if they needed Claude, he was always there."

"Anytime there was a dispute or disagreement over the interpretation of a particular part of the Bible or other differences within the church, Claude would listen to all sides, but he stood by what he believed. He felt that worship services should be orderly and respectful. He was always thoughtful of his congregation and tried to maintain a schedule for beginning and ending his services. He believed in the two ordinances of the church — baptism and the Lord's Supper — missions, training programs, and the efforts of the Baptist Convention. He believed the Bible cover to cover and spoke its message as God's words to us."

During the fifty-five years of his ministry to the families in the five counties of northeast Georgia, Claude has shared long, deep friendships with many of them. To these families, he has been one of their own. He has been there to celebrate the joy of birth, baptized new converts, rejoiced at the conversions of souls to God, pronounced the wedding vows, and shared the sorrow and felt the pain when God has taken their loved ones home. One man related the reasons for his long standing affection for Claude this way:

Claude at Mt. View in 1984.

"He baptized my mother and my daddy, he baptized me and my wife, he baptized my brother and my sister, my nieces and nephews, my boy and my girls, and he married me and my wife. He married my brother and my sister, my son and my daughters, and my nephew. He preached my mother, daddy, and brother's funerals. I went to school with him, and he spent many nights in our home with us when I was a boy. He's lasted so long because of his friendly personality and his dedication. And he's always lived what he preached. I've always said that if I was hunting a good man, I wouldn't pass up Claude Hood's house."

One woman who was interviewed expressed her thoughts as follows:

"I was just a little girl when Claude came to our church. He was the first minister that I knew who visited in the community, especially the sick. There's no telling how many cars he has worn out. When he first came most folks still came to church in wagons. They would bring quilts and spread them under the benches for the babies to sleep on.

During revivals the church would be packed. Chairs would be put in the aisles and there would still be a yard full that could not get into the church. Claude was so special, so loving and kind. There wasn't anything he wouldn't do for you. He was always there for us. Everybody wanted him to go home with them, so we had to pass him around. He baptized me and most of my brothers and sisters. He married all of us but one. Mama would say, 'He always listened to your every request and followed through with it.' My grandma loved him like a son. She would send for him or write him a letter when she wanted him to help pray for someone.

Claude was single when he came to our church, but when he did marry, she was so kind and sweet. She was very quiet and didn't say much, but she was always by his side. They have both been there when we were saved, baptized, married, in sickness and health, also during the good and bad times. Our community is a better place to live by their having been at our church. We sure do love them."

Leroy Conner (deceased) and Claude. 1940's.

A long-time friend who moved from the mountain area commented:

"Claude came across as a man with a message. He has had a tremendous impact on that part of the state (Northeast Georgia) during his ministry."

The term "pass the hat" comes from the days when the offering for the pastor was actually collected in a hat. Claude never discussed his salary with a pulpit committee before deciding whether to take a church. In the early days of his ministry, whenever the members decided they wanted to give the preacher some money, one member would take his hat and go around the congregation to accept the money people wanted to give. Sometimes there were only a few pennies or maybe a dime. One year a dollar was paid by a church for the entire year's salary, including revival. The next year it increased by 100 percent, to two dollars! The minutes of one church show that in the late 1930's, it was moved, seconded, and voted that each member of the church try to pay the pastor at least one dollar during the year.

In the mid-1950's, the records of a particular church show their offering to Claude being as low as $9.75 one month and a high of $31.82 another month. The revival offering of $70.50 was either split or given in full to the visiting preacher. Claude's total salary from that church for the year was $315. This was for two Sunday morning services, conference once during the month, and visiting the sick, preaching funerals, the revival, and any other services for which he was needed. Another church he pastored during the 1950's paid $30 per month. In 1954, Claude's average weekly income from five churches was $59.55 each week, and this was to cover all his expenses.

Claude has always gone whenever and wherever he was asked...for love...not for pay. He has never depended solely upon his ministry or his churches for financial support of himself and his family, although many people have been most kind and generous to him with various kinds of support over the years. Because of this help, along with his and Edna's hard work on their farm and in their home, he has always been able to be where he was needed in churches, funerals, visiting or providing transportation for those who needed it. He has also given his tithe (10 percent of his earnings) back to the church every year since his ministry began.

The most meaningful gifts or offerings have often come from those who had little to give, but asked him to accept their small gift to help someone else. Sometimes in the earlier days he would be given money when he went home with a family to share a meal. It was the custom of some families to turn the dinner plate upside down on the table until time to serve the meal. Sometimes when Claude would turn his plate over he would find a few coins had been placed under it for him. This always touched him very much, because although it might have been only a small amount, it represented a big sacrifice on the part of the giver, who was often poor and did not really have even a few cents to spare. It was truly a gift of love.

During all Claude's years of working with churches, he has always tried not to show any difference in the treatment of any individual or family because of money or position. If there has been any difference it has been to do more for those individuals who have had less (material possessions). He always visited the families of the poor as well as those who had greater wealth. When questioned about his preference in working with various age groups, Claude responded that he tried not to show any difference between the young people and older adults; one was as precious as the other. He said, "I always had respect for older people, and I wanted to help the young people. The middle age group were usually able to take care of themselves."

When folks still walked most places they went, they walked to their homes together after the night services of revivals. Sometimes when it rained they pulled off their shoes and walked barefoot so they would not get their shoes muddy. When they got home they washed their feet, and then sometimes they would stay up until midnight or later enjoying long conversations about various topics. There were no televisions, and few radios, so people engaged in the art of conversation, that is to say they enjoyed talking and sharing their thoughts and opinions with each other.

In his younger days Claude enjoyed playing practical jokes on his friends and teasing them. Rev. Clifford Palmer (now deceased) helped Claude in several revivals during his early ministry, and he was also a good friend. They traveled together to many churches and stayed overnight in the homes of many members of their congregations. Spending so much time together, there was ample opportunity to play practical jokes on each other.

Usually the preachers were given their own room, but they had to share a bed. One particular night Claude was awakened by Cliff's snoring. Since Claude was unable to go back to sleep because of the "noise," he decided to do something to stop it. Claude had (what he thought) was a bright idea. He would use his pillow to rouse Cliff and maybe stop him from snoring. Actually, he meant to hit Cliff across the head with it; however, somewhere in the planning process, Claude made a mistake in his calculations. Just as Claude raised the pillow over his head, Cliff somehow swiftly drew his knees up to his chest and kicked Claude out of the bed and into the middle of the floor! Of course this awakened everyone in the house, and they all rushed in to see what the "racket" (noise) was. What they found was Claude sitting in the middle of the floor, pillow in hand, and Cliff sitting in bed laughing at him. 'Til this day, Claude still wonders how Cliff could have been so soundly asleep, completely covered, and yet have been able to kick him out of the bed, pillow and all, before he could get in one lick. Over the years, the two of them had many good laughs over the stunt.

Another time Claude and Cliff were in revival and were spending the night with a long-time friend. There was a bed in the living room (or the fireplace room) that was used for company. Claude and Cliff were to sleep there. The husband and wife had already retired to their room and gone to bed. Later they were awakened by someone laughing. Then in a short time they heard other strange sounds and got up to see what all of the "commotion" was about. When they walked into the room Cliff was chasing Claude 'round and 'round the bed. Cliff had gone outside (to the bathroom), and while he was gone Claude blew out the light, so Cliff could not see how to get back inside. When Cliff finally felt his way back inside, he jerked Claude out of the bed and gave him several good licks with his belt before Claude could get away. Claude said, "It was a high, four poster bed, and I tried to hide behind the headboard, but he kept whipping me around the bed. I don't know how many licks he gave me before he settled down, but it was all in fun." At still another time, they had a feather pillow fight which caused considerable damage to the feather pillows.

Claude walked to his churches for two years, but finally realized he had to have an automobile in order to serve his members and pastor the churches as he felt he should. So in 1934, he borrowed $500 to buy his first car; a 1927 Chevrolet. Later he bought a 1929 Chevrolet, and then a 1931 Roadster. His first Ford was a two door, 1936 Model "A", in black of course. He had a 1940 Ford Coup in 1944, and soon thereafter, he bought his only Studebaker.

Not long after he had bought his first car, Claude was driving down the road one afternoon, when he came upon a friend walking down the road. Claude knew the friend did not recognize him, so he decided to tease him by pretending he was going to run over him. At this time there were few cars in rural parts of the counties, so the roads were not crowded, and there was plenty of room for those walking as well as any automobiles. As Claude drove his car closer and closer, his friend kept getting further off the road until he was completely in the ditch. The only place for the friend to get away from this crazy driver was up a bank. Finally, when the car was close enough, Claude was recognized. The friend laughingly tells the story and says, "Finally I just stopped and sulled (refused to move). So Claude came on up and said, 'Get in if you wanna ride,' and of course I did. It saved me having to walk all the way to my house." The friend invited Claude to come in, have supper, and spend the night, and he accepted. As it turned out, left-overs were being served for supper. They had cornbread, peas and milk. The friend's wife was embarrassed, but her husband said, "Lordy mercy, Claude can eat it one time, if we eat it all the time." Those are the times which Claude remembers most fondly; the times when he was treated as "one of the family" by his friends.

In 1940, Claude began dating Edna Burke of Clarkesville, Georgia. Dating had to be worked into his busy schedule whenever there was any free time. Since most churches did not have services on Saturday or Sunday nights, he usually was able to schedule their dates on Saturday or Sunday afternoons. At that time the Cleveland/Clarkesville Road was still unpaved and travel during rainy weather and snow was difficult. He made the trip many times during the four years they dated, when mud would be up to the axel of his car, and other cars would be sitting along the roadside, stuck in the mud.

After dating for four years, they decided to get married, but planned to keep the marriage a secret for awhile. Claude's dad was building them a house on his farm in White County, and it was still under construction, so they decided not to announce the marriage until they could move into their new house. Claude had known the Burke family for several years before he ever dated Edna, and although her dad had always thought very highly of Claude over the years, when he realized that Claude might marry his youngest daughter he became less fond of him. He was not ready to give up his baby, even though she was 21, nor did he really want a preacher for a son-in-law. Since it was doubtful that Edna's dad would give his consent to the marriage, the couple decided to elope. An aunt and uncle of Edna's attended the wedding as witnesses. Not only was Edna very special to them, but they were also fond of Claude. He had served as the pastor of their church in Habersham County for several years.

So the secret wedding was planned, and Rev. Garnett Campbell, pastor of Tesnatee Baptist Church was going to meet them at the church on Saturday night to marry them. Edna's aunt, uncle and a close friend carried her to the church to meet Claude and Rev. Campbell. The wedding party, having arrived, made their way to the front door of the church to go in for the ceremony. However, one minor detail which created a major problem, had been overlooked. The door of the church was locked, and no one at the wedding had a key to unlock it. At first the idea of using car lights was considered, but someone might see the cars and come to investigate, and after all, this was supposed to be a secret wedding. So with that idea ruled out, there was only the moonlight. Fortunately the evening was wonderfully romantic with a beautiful full moon, and there was enough light to see how to read the wedding ceremony. Rev. Campbell was not accustomed to improvising a church, altar, lighting, and the ceremony as well. So, by the time the ceremony began he was very nervous. He proceeded with no major problems until he got to the ring ceremony. Then for whatever reason, he could no longer see how to read the ceremony. Having been in the ministry for twelve years and having married many people, Claude of course knew the ceremony. Without hesitation, Claude did the only thing any ordained minister would do in this circumstance, he left his bride standing there alone and went up and finished reading his own wedding ceremony! He has read many wedding ceremonies since, but none have compared to the one he read that night while standing on the little knoll in White County, in the moonlight on September 2, 1944.

Edna and Claude in 1944, shortly after they were married.

Over the next few weeks as word of their marriage became known, Edna moved from her parents' home in Clarkesville. She and Claude lived with his mother and dad until their house was completed several weeks later. Only one year later they left their new house to move to Gainesville, Georgia, where Claude had accepted the pastorship of Westside Baptist Church. While in Gainesville they built a house on the Cleveland Road in the New Bridge Community and lived there for approximately five years before moving back to White County.

"Home is where the heart is."

Edna in 1946, at the house used as the pastorium for Westside Church in Gainesville, Georgia.

Claude and Edna's first house, built in 1944, in the Mt. View Community, near Cleveland, Georgia.

Claude and Edna had this house built in Gainesville in 1947.

Built in 1975, this house is where Claude and Edna presently live on their farm in the Mossy Creek District of White County.

"A house becomes a home."

Claude and Edna bought the Dillard Cooley Place on Old Highway 129 in 1952, and continued living there until 1975. The house is over 100 years old.

One of Claude's fields under cultivation was used as an experimental project of the U. S. Department of Agriculture in 1956. The farm was divided by highway 129, with Claude owning the property on both sides. (Soil Conservation Photo)

The Ministerial Years

In 1952, Claude bought the Dillard Cooley Place on Mossy Creek, near what was earlier in the century, the Mel-Dean Train Station. The old homeplace was said to be well over one hundred years old. In the late 1970's, the house and part of the farm were sold, and Claude and Edna built a new house on the remaining property where they live today.

Edna's marriage to Claude brought with it a whole new lifestyle for her: one which required her to be on the go most of the time meeting and working with people who were strangers to her. There was also adjusting to the full reality that Claude's commitment to his ministry came first, and family plans and functions had to be changed accordingly. In those days, and often today, wherever they went, people knew Claude, so as word spread of his marriage Edna became the center of attention. Since Claude had been a well-known, eligible bachelor for many years, everyone wanted to see and meet his new wife.

Eula Holland Savage, Myrtice Holland Foster (l-r), Edna, and Claude, in 1944.

During the following months and years, Edna soon found, as Claude already knew, that wherever he went in his official capacity as a minister, he and his family were in the spotlight. Any action taken by a public figure is always either applauded or criticized. Then, as now, it is impossible to please everyone.

Throughout their ministry, Claude and Edna's loyal friends and supporters who stood by them were a much-needed source of strength and inspiration to continue in God's work during the good times and during the persecution and criticism, which also came with the job. The life of a minister was sometimes painful and discouraging. Although similar problems could be found in any setting involving people, it seemed that getting a church congregation to reach an agreement and cooperate in a Christian manner could sometimes be most difficult. But then, there were the good times when no sweeter spirit could be found than in the congregation of a Christian church.

Eating and sleeping in the homes of people she didn't know was a new experience for Edna. The first time she stayed overnight in the home of one of their church members was during a summer revival. She had her first encounter with bedbugs during that week. They were so bad that she and Claude sat up all night in straight-backed, wooden chairs (which were the only kind of chairs in their room) with the oil lamp burning so they would not be bitten. There was a spinning wheel in the bedroom and Edna says, "The bedbugs marched around and around that wheel all night while we sat there using each other as a prop to keep from falling out of the chairs if we fell asleep. We knew that we couldn't say anything the next morning to the folks we were staying with, so we tried to make the best of it."

The next day at church the service ran a little longer than normal, and Claude was concerned about Edna's having not gotten any rest the night before, so he decided to send her on ahead with the family where they were to have lunch and spend that night. He told her to go on to bed, and try to get some rest that afternoon. Upon arrival at the home she was graciously welcomed and provided with the best that they had. By this time she was very tired and prepared to rest for an hour or so. She turned down the cover on the bed, and "low and behold" (sure enough) the bed was covered with bedbugs! When Claude arrived, Edna told him what she had found in the bed. After a late lunch, they thanked their host for the hospitality and explained they would not be staying overnight, because they needed to go back home that night. Bedbugs were a new experience for Edna, as they had been for Claude years earlier. Edna's family never had bedbugs, but she still remembers her encounters with them when visiting in other homes.

Rev. Willis Pruitt of Athens, Georgia, assisted Claude in several revivals during the 1950's. He had so many battles with bedbugs during his ministry that he often joked about his relationship with them. He would laugh and say that he was sure the bedbugs knew him personally and sang with joy when they saw him coming to visit. Since he loved the old hymns, he knew that the bedbugs did too. He would tell of their imagined favorites being sung in this refrain:

As he came into the house: *"When the Saints Go Marching In"* As he started to climb the stairs: *"Onward Christian Soldiers"* As he laid down on the bed: *"There Is A Fountain Filled With Blood"* As he left the house: *"God Be With You 'Till We Meet Again."*

Although some of the problems can be laughed about today, bedbugs were a nuisance, and ridding a house of them was most difficult.

During the weeks when Claude assisted in revivals at other churches, he and Edna went home with the people according to the schedule arranged by the pastor of the church. In their own church, they made every effort not to show partiality, by visiting and eating in the homes of all members who invited them. Sharing meals with families could sometimes present unique challenges. In earlier days, Claude had a strong stomach and could eat most anything. In fact, he made a special effort to do so when he was a guest in someone's home; but once when he stayed overnight with an older couple, he had a situation occur that got the best of him after breakfast. That morning when his eggs were served, there was a big blow-fly stuck on one of them. The lady could not, or did not, see it. He recalls eating some of the other food, and then excusing himself quickly. He lost his breakfast, but he never let the man and woman know it. He said she would have been so upset, because in her younger days she had been a very good, clean cook. There were no refrigerators and freezers and no plastic containers and wraps, so preserving food in those days was difficult.

When visiting in someone's home, Claude was usually asked to give a blessing before the meal was served. Edna enjoys teasing Claude about his blessings because she says he was always thankful for the good food that had been prepared for them before he knew whether it was good or not. Edna would often help in the kitchen, and sometimes seeing how the food had been prepared, she knew when Claude should have reworded his blessing. For example, once she was told to get a cake out of a pie safe. When she opened the doors on the safe, the cake had rat droppings on it. She managed to get a knife and remove that part of the icing by saying something had smudged the icing, and that it needed to be smoothed. When careful thought is given to that statement, it could be true — she did not lie — but as the old saying goes, she did probably "beat the devil around the bush." The truth was stretched somewhat, in the name of a good deed.

Another time there were ants in a pie to be served, but she somehow managed to remove them and save most of the pie. Claude would usually not know about these things until they were on their way home, which was probably fortunate, because it allowed him to be sincere and honest in his compliments to the cook.

Once when visiting a family for dinner, Claude and Edna were told that the man of the house would not be able to be with them because he had to attend to some pressing business in town. Edna was sent to the spring house (the place where milk and other foods were kept in the stream to be kept cool) with one of the daughters to get the milk. When they reached the spring house, they found the girl's dad propped against a tree. He was passed-out from being drunk. The young girl explained that her mother wanted Preacher Claude to come and eat with them so much, and she was ashamed to tell him that her husband was off on another one of his drunks. Therefore, the family had decided to say that he was away and hoped he did not decide to come home until Claude and Edna had left. Edna and the young girl picked up the milk, returned to the house, and never mentioned seeing anyone. Later, Edna told Claude of the encounter.

Claude and Edna were two very gracious people who would never do or say anything to cause embarrassment or hurt to anyone if they could help it. Some people would simply just have refused to eat the food, or told the hostess there was something wrong with it. Claude and Edna Hood would never do that. They knew how much pride people took in preparing the best that they had when the preacher came to visit. Once they went home with a family for dinner and only had spoons to eat with. The family was very poor and had not bought any other pieces of silver except kitchen knives and cooking spoons. Everyone enjoyed the meal and the visit, and no apologies or mention was ever made of the spoons. Special efforts were made by those church members who did not invite them to their homes on a regular basis. If there were problems in the home of someone whom they knew well, they were more often treated like a part of the family, and the atmosphere was more relaxed. But whatever the situation, Claude and Edna have always tried to consider the feelings of others.

For every bad experience during their ministry there are hundreds of great ones. They have enjoyed great times, lots of fun, made lasting friendships, and been treated to some of the best country cooking anywhere! The southern, country cooking of those days is certainly not popular to most members of today's health-conscious, younger generations, but nothing can ever take the place of the flavors and the seasonings of good country cooking, regardless of how unhealthy it is deemed by today's standards of food preparation.

As Christmases have come and gone, Claude and Edna have received some strange gifts, but one was particularly different. This gift box was beautifully wrapped, but when Edna opened it, she found a rabbit, cleaned and ready to be cooked. It was not meant as a joke. One of their members raised them commercially for eating. This was his special gift to them. Another time Claude was given a pig as a Christmas gift. It was not wrapped, however, and was alive. One Sunday morning a few months later, the pig escaped from its pen. This was a double problem, because it was time for Claude to leave for church. He knew that if he left without catching the pig and putting it back in the pen, he would never see it again. So he tried and tried to catch it. It kept getting away, but he was determined to catch it before he quit. He chased it down into a branch (stream) and finally caught it in the water. Needless to say, the pig chase made him late for church that morning. It was one of a very few times that he was ever late to a service. Upon arriving at the church, he told the Sunday School Superintendent about his problems that morning, and then they went into the church for the worship service. When the Superintendent finished giving his Sunday School Report, he said, "I thought you all would like to know the reason the preacher missed Sunday School today was because he had to baptize his pig this morning before he could come to church." He just left it at that. So Claude had to explain to the congregation that he was not really baptizing his pig; he was just catching it. He was teased about baptizing the pig for months after that episode.

Since there were few automobiles in the rural mountain communities, those who had automobiles often tried to help with sickness and emergencies by "carrying" (transporting) people to doctors, hospitals, jails, and prisons. Claude was often asked to drive folks to visit their family members at different places. Also, Claude usually picked up one or two families (depending on the numbers) on his way to church services in the various communities. There were always some families with children who needed to be in church, but did not have a car, and it was too far for them to walk. Having only one daughter, there was plenty of room left in his car for other families to ride to church with them.

Since he began his ministry fifty-five years ago, Claude has made it a part of his daily life to find a place three times each day where he can be alone to offer a quiet prayer to God. The only time he has not kept this schedule has been when he was physically unable to do so due to sickness. He feels it is important to make time during the busy day to stop, even for just a moment, and speak to God or to listen as He speaks.

Claude has depended upon God to give him the message he is to deliver, and God has not failed to do so. The day he made his commitment to the ministry, he placed his body and soul completely in God's hands, and God has always provided food, clothing and shelter for his body, and strength for his soul. Claude often quotes Psalms 23:1, *"The Lord is my Shepherd; I shall not want."* Claude believes this with all of his heart, and God has never failed him in this promise.

To further tell of his belief, there is a quote that has become synonymous with Claude. It has become his message in a statement of fact and his plea to all who will hear: *"If you miss Heaven, you've missed it all!"*

For the example he has set, the life he has led, and the lives he has touched, The Reverend Claude Edward Hood will leave the part of the world that has been touched by his life a far better place because he was here. His impact may seem small compared to one that has influenced a nation or the world, but if each individual assumed as much responsibility for his fellowman and the small part of the world which he touches, just think of what could be accomplished.

The legacy Claude Hood will leave for those who follow him will be his sincere belief that God gives each individual the ability and the opportunity to make a difference in their world, however large or small the realm of that world is. One person can make the world a better place.

8-A The Daily Times, Gainesville, Ga., Monday, August 14, 1972

Claude Hood

Reception honors self-made preacher

By LETRELL SIMPSON
Special To The Times

In July 1932, when the Rev. Claude Hood received his calling to the ministry, he was a young man of 22 filled with doubts who questioned his ability to deliver the Word of God. Forty years later he still humbly doubts his abilities as a minister, but his record indicates that he stands alone with his doubts.

Oldtimers might refer to Mr. Hood as a self-made preacher. Because his father needed him to work on their White County farm, the Baptist minister made it through only the sixth grade when he was 17, and he became embarrassed at his age following his call to the ministry at the age of 25, he enrolled at the Clarkesville School and four years later graduated from Cleveland High.

The modest six-footer, speaking in his quiet, calm voice told how Governor Hardman visited his church at Amos Creek one Sunday morning and heard him preach. Mr. Hood confessed that he tried to get the governor to make a talk, hoping he would not have to preach with him in the congregation, but the governor would have no part in such a scheme. He later received a letter from the governor, encouraging him to enroll at Mercer University and informing him that he would help him secure funds for his education. Mr. Hood said that although he had to write the governor and tell him he was not eligible for college because he did not finish high school, this gave him the incentive and the courage to enroll in the seventh grade at the age of 25.

During the four years he was in classroom, he pastored four and five churches and tells today how he often had to leave school to preach a funeral or help with a revival. Obviously his ministerial work did not interfere, however, because he completed his five years of study in four. He later completed numerous courses at Truett McConnell, Mercer University and the University of Georgia.

Looking back into the early years of his ministry, the pastor of New Bridge Baptist Church recalled how he often walked to his waiting congregations. He told of fording creeks and how on one occasion he pulled off his socks to wade the creek and left them in his pocket. Later while delivering his sermon in front of "college students and the likes," he remembered he still had the socks in his pocket. On another occasion, when he had preached an early sermon and walked to his next appointment, he ran late and half of the congregation left, deciding there would not be preaching that Sunday.

It was not uncommon for preachers to accommodate several churches when Mr. Hood began his preaching. He often served four or five churches and at one time pastored five part-time and one fulltime church. When questioned about his schedule, the stylishly dressed minister hesitated for fear he might sound boastful, and it was only after encouragement that he explained the congregation wanted him as their pastor and hired an assistant to fill in on the Sundays he was obligated to other churches.

Squeezed into these busy days he served as a trustee on the White County Board of Education and as chaplain in both the Senate and the House of Representatives. Considering that he has averaged at least one funeral each week in his 40 years in the ministry, along with weddings and some marriage counseling on the side, Mr. Hood's life exemplifies the kind of man he is, and why today he is often called from the various 27 churches he has pastored to assist their church and their families in times of sorrow and in times of happiness.

Always waiting for a quick, easy grin to slide across his face, he tells how he baptized his wife when she was 14 and later when he was called to pastor her church the second time, he married the former Miss Edna Burke of Clarkesville.

When questioned about his role as a family man and as a minister, his wife and daughter chimed in to report that his dedication always cut vacations short because he refused to be gone on Sundays, and Mrs. Hood laughingly recalled packing a picnic lunch three separate times before they finally made it out of the house away from the ring of the telephone.

Mr. Hood sees the changing in the times as playing a particular role in his life. "When I started out we had baptizings in the nearest creek or river and folks came from miles around," he explained. He recalled baptizing 45 newly-proclaimed Christians at Mount View, his home church, and he baptized 36 in a muddy fish pond near Holly Springs. He remembers that he once preached 50 nights straight without interruption and has known the joy of baptizing a 71-year-old woman and a 76-year-old man. In addition to baptizing his wife at the age of 14, he baptized his daughter at the age of 9.

Emphasizing again his role as a family man and how he had to sandwich in time for his private life, the preacher told of one day when he preached a funeral at 11 a.m., a wedding at 1 p.m., funerals again at 2 and 3:30 and conducted a conference meeting at 7:30.

It has been a full, rich life for the minister who pastored Mount View for 29 years and is in his 11th year at New Bridge, and he is quick to point out that it would have been an impossible task had it not been for God in his life. A man who has preached thousands of sermons but has never prepared a note, he says he puts his faith in God to help him to deliver what he feels in his heart. "I have always been proud to serve," the preacher explained, "especially in sorrow, because you never know when your hour will come."

A reception in his honor yesterday was something Claude Hood says he could have lived without, but it provided folks of long ago and those who know him today an opportunity to show their appreciation to a man who has cared so long for them.

Weddings

A wedding is a joyful celebration of tradition. Claude has married hundreds of couples during his ministry. Many times he has married a couple and years later married their children.

Bessie Farmer to Euell Keith, circa 1940.

Joan Young to J. W. Seabolt, circa 1957.

Buell Keith to Bill Jones, December 20, 1952.

Weddings

Hilda Gilleland marries in 1967.

Tina Black (Claude's great niece) marries Stuart Stovall at the First Baptist Church in Cleveland, Georgia, in 1986.

Cliff Smallwood to Pauline Whitmire, circa 1962.

Claude at a Mt. View Baptist Church wedding, 1960's.

Community Involvement

Claude served as Chaplain for the House of Representatives while Tom was a State Representative, circa 1961. Pictured are (back row, l-r) Claude, Edna, Mildred and Tom Hood; (front row, l-r) Claudette, Graham Hood telling Governor Ernest Vandiver (1959-1963) how old he is, and Beverly Hood.

Members of Masonic Yonah Lodge No. 382, received 25-year membership pins in 1973. Pictured are (l-r): H. A. Allison, Wilson Dyer (deceased), Thomas Glover, Claude Hood, George Johnson (deceased), Ralph Pardue (deceased), Frank Russell, Graves Westmoreland (deceased), Marvin Westmoreland (deceased), Roy Powers (deceased), and John Burgess who presented the pins.

Community

Claude served on the Board of Trustees for the White County Board of Education from 1959-1964. Pictured (front row, l-r) are: J. L. Nix, Clarence Cooley, and Ed Head. (back row, l-r) George McCollum, Claude, and Lee Mize.

Claude (left) as Chaplain of the House of Representatives.

While pastor of New Bridge Church, Claude worked with Ty Bishop (left) in earning the rank of Eagle Scout. Circa 1972.

The Claude E. Hood Family

Claude and Edna have one daughter, Edna Claudette, born April 1, 1947.

Claude, Edna and Claudette (1 yr. old), 1948.

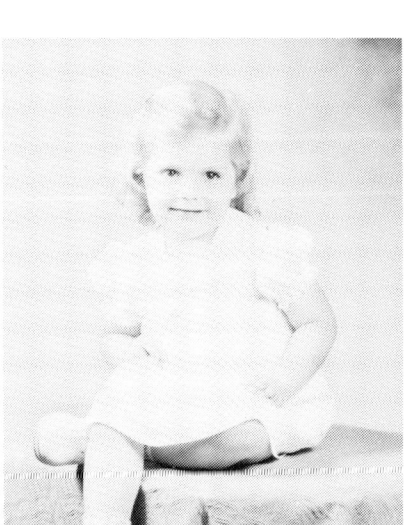
Claudette, four years old.

Edna and Claude, with Claudette at six months.

Claudette Hood Howell, author, THE TIME WAS.

Claude dealing with the "terrible-two's."

Claude and his grandson

Claude and Edna have one grandson, Craig Austin, born March 26, 1967, and one step-granddaughter, Susan, born November 7, 1964.

Craig (1 yr. old) and Claude, 1968.

Craig (5 years old) tries out his grandfather's new rocker, a gift from New Bridge Baptist Church, on Claude's 40th Anniversary in the ministry.

Robert and Susan with Claude and Edna in 1982.

In 1983 Claude and Craig were cutting holly from a tree on a creek bank, when Craig fell into the water. Everyone got quite a laugh!

As Time Passes...
Three Generations

Edna, Claude, Claudette, and Craig in 1972.

Craig, Claude, Edna, and Claudette in 1984. Appreciation Day at Mt. View Baptist Church honoring Claude's 50 years of ministry.

Claudette Hood and Robert N. Howell Family

Robert, Claudette, Susan, and Craig, 1977.

Pictured on the front row are Claudette and Craig, with Robert and Susan, 1987.

Craig with his trumpet, 1986.

Susan in 1985.

On The Lighter Side...
Relaxation

Vacation in St. Augustine, Florida during the late 1950's.

An outing in the 1950's. Claude (left) and Rev. Harry Ragan.

Visiting the Cherokee Indian Reservation in the 1950's are Edna, Claudette, and Claude.

Claude enjoys a fishing trip to Nottely Lake in Blairsville, Georgia, with Claudette (left) and Joyce Ragan Robinson. Circa 1959.

Claude on a fishing trip with the late A. R. Fletcher.

Funeral Customs

In the late 19th century and early 20th century, the majority of deaths occurred in the home. If a person died elsewhere, the body was returned home as quickly as possible. The home was the central point of mourning. A hush would fall over the household, blinds would be drawn, people would walk about on tiptoe, and words were spoken in hushed tones.

Upon the pronouncement of death, the women closed the eyes of the deceased and straightened his or her limbs. If the dead person had false teeth, these were quickly placed back into the mouth. Rural folks traditionally accepted the responsibilities of preparing the body of their family member for burial.

As early as 1880, in some larger towns, the option of taking the body to the funeral parlor was available. However, as late as 1910, it was thought that the funeral parlor was used for people who had no home of their own or had no relatives or friends who would offer the use of their home. In rural areas, even after undertakers began taking the body to the funeral parlor to be embalmed, the family insisted upon bringing it back home as soon as possible. Years later, the funeral parlor came to be called a funeral "home," as they were more readily accepted and used by families for receiving friends and viewing of the body of the deceased, thus changing years of tradition.

If the body was not buried within one day, preservation measures would be needed; however, embalming was not always the method selected. In fact, the family had two choices: the body could be kept in a cooler or "corpse preserver," which was surrounded with ice until the funeral; or, the undertaker could embalm the body with chemicals. Some of the corpse preservers were made so the remains could be viewed through a small glass window on the top of the coffin. To maintain the low temperature, it was necessary for the lid of the coffin to remain closed.

In rural areas and small towns the news of death spread rapidly. Relatives, neighbors, and friends usually became involved in the care and/or disposition of the body and in the support and help given the bereaved family. The body was "laid out" either by the family or by persons in the community who had experience in these matters. The body was washed and dressed in a favorite dress or suit, then moved from the bedroom to the parlor for viewing sometimes before the coffin was brought to the house. Friends and neighbors came to pay their last respects upon hearing of the "passing." Members of the deceased's family would be seated in the living room to receive condolences. Each caller walked quietly into the parlor to see the corpse, as everyone was expected to do, and then each commented on how natural and peaceful it looked, which was also expected.

Members of the community would "set up" all night, making sure that the family was not alone in their time of bereavement. Customs varied by communities as to whether or not food was prepared by neighbors and taken to the home to help serve the friends and relatives gathered there. It was also customary to provide coffee and snacks for those who kept the watch during the night.

After preserving the body by embalming became a commonplace custom, the funeral would sometimes not be held for two or three days after death, so, it became necessary for the relatives and neighbors to rotate the responsibility to "set up" for several nights.

Usually one individual in each community was widely known for his abilities to build coffins and kept the necessary supplies in his home. One builder stored the white pine lumber in the rafters of his kitchen over the cook stove to keep them dry. Folks would send for him, and he would take the lumber and his tools to the home of the deceased, where he would make the coffin. Sometimes it would take all night. Then, the next morning he would go to the graveyard, help dig the grave, and stay for the funeral before going back home. He often traveled many miles to other communities to make the coffins.

The coffin gradually came to be called a casket, thus softening the term somewhat. If the family preferred to have a "bought" casket, they could usually go to the furniture store in town to select one. It was a common practice in the early days of North Georgia towns for the furniture dealer to also be the undertaker. The casket might not yet be lined or "trimmed," and the furniture dealer and his wife often did this to complete it. Those folks who could not afford to buy a casket could purchase just the handles and the trimmings for their home-made one. The funeral parlor was usually located adjacent to, or upstairs over, the furniture store. A parlor or sitting room was available for use by the family of the deceased when there was a need.

Griffin Brothers Furniture and Casket Store, Clermont, GA. In 1920, caskets and burial supplies were sold at the furniture store. (Georgia Department of Archives and History.)

As funeral homes have physically changed over the years, so have the services they provide to families. They have gone from being located in houses, to today's look of a more business-like setting. With this new expansion has come an added service, for those who elect to use it, the funeral home chapel. For any number of reasons, a family may elect to use the chapel instead of going to a church for the funeral.

Funeral Customs

Usually in smaller communities, the funeral "homes" are still being used. All of these changes are positive improvements from the days when the funeral home was called the "mortuary."

A noticeable difference can be seen in the markers of earlier years and today's simple marker, which may only have the deceased's name, birth and death dates written on it. In the earliest days, a simple slab marker was all that was available or affordable. Then the headstones became very individualized both in size, shape, and inscription. Often, much can be learned about the deceased's life by reading the inscriptions on the headstones or "tombstones."

Vickers Funeral Home was located on West Broad Street, in Gainesville, GA. This large structure was typical of funeral homes of the time. It was said to have been built by Harvey Hall, before the Civil War, and later owned by a Mr. Findley. In 1933, Hubert Vickers purchased the house and used it as a funeral home. It continued being used as a funeral home after it was purchased by William R. Strickland. The building was torn down in 1987. (Georgia Department of Archives and History.)

The gravestone of W. Ed Hood and Rosa Hood (Claude's grandparents). They are buried in the cemetery where Hood's Chapel was once located. Note the inscriptions. This type of marker was very common earlier in the century.

In the United States, the idea of embalming had been around since the time of the Civil War; yet, many people feared the process, as they thought it required mutilation of the deceased's body. Also, they were not sure it was the "Christian" thing to do, and most opposition was probably based on the fear of the unknown.

If the family raised too much objection against embalming, a family member, or close friend of the family, was allowed to watch the process to insure that no mutilation took place. When the observer saw the size of the small incision made to facilitate the process, he was generally satisfied and seldom remained to witness the balance of the embalming procedure.

If the undertaker had training in chemical embalming, he undoubtedly defended its humaneness and pointed to all its obvious advantages over ice-cooling: sanitation; duration; reliability; and simplicity. The possibility of an iced-cooled corpse decomposing rapidly, once taken out of the "preserver," could neither be ignored nor overlooked. Prices, either way, did not vary greatly at the time, but chemical embalming, on the whole, tended to be a little more expensive.

SEARS, ROEBUCK & CO. (Inc.), Cheapest Supply House on Earth, Chicago. CATALOGUE No. 110. 739

MEMORIAL DEPARTMENT

THE WORLD'S BEST ROYAL BLUE VERMONT MARBLE. IT IS EVERYWHERE CONCEDED TO BE THE FINEST IN THE WORLD. It is of rich, unfading color, and superior to the other blue marbles on the market which lose their color on exposure to the weather. **A FINE, CLOSE GRAINED MARBLE.**

OUR SUPERIOR FINISHING. We do not use Oxalic Acid, and we employ only skilled artisans. We do not have our work done by the piece, but only employ day labor, thus securing the best possible fineness in finish.
WE OFFER YOU the handsome Marble Markers shown on these pages, with any lettering you desire, at half the prices you can buy them from your nearest marble dealer, and **WE PAY THE FREIGHT** east of the Rocky Mountains.

OUR LIBERAL $1.00 C. O. D. OFFER. Send us any lettering you may desire carved in the marble, and $1.00 as a guarantee of good faith, and we will send you, freight prepaid, any tombstone you may select from these pages. If it is not exactly as represented and the lettering handsomely engraved according to your instructions, you can return it to us and we will refund the money. Examine it at your freight depot, and if satisfactory, pay the agent our catalogue price less the $1.00 sent with order.

UNHEARD OF VALUE AT $29.00 AND UPWARDS.

LIKE EVERY ONE of our higher grade tombstones this monument is made in the same famous quarry, and, by reason of having been made there, you are guaranteed a quality which you might not expect anywhere else.
The measurements of the smaller size of this tombstone are as follows: Bottom base, 1 foot 4 inches, by 1 foot 4 inches, by 8 inches. Base, 1 foot, by 1 foot, by 6 inches. Shaft, 2 feet 6 inches, by 8 inches, by 8 inches. Height over all, 3 feet 8 inches.
This tombstone is made in the following variety and qualities of marble:

No. 42755	Dark vein marble	$29.00
No. 42756	Florence No. 2	29.00
No. 42757	Dark mottled marble	31.25
No. 42758	Extra dark vein marble	31.25
No. 42759	Average Florence marble	31.25
No. 42760	Extra dark mottled marble	33.00
No. 42761	Florence No. 1	33.00

A LARGER SIZE AT $46.75 TO $52.50.

The next largest size of this handsome monument is as follows: Bottom base, 1 foot 6 inches, by 1 foot 6 inches, by 10 inches. Base, 1 foot 2 inches, by 1 foot 2 inches, by 8 inches. Shaft, 2 feet 10 inches, by 10 inches, by 10 inches. Height over all, 4 feet 4 inches. Our special prices on this size are as follows:

No. 42762	Dark vein marble	$46.75
No. 42763	Florence No. 2	46.75
No. 42764	Dark mottled marble	50.00
No. 42765	Extra dark vein marble	50.00
No. 42766	Average Florence marble	50.00
No. 42767	Extra dark mottled marble	52.50
No. 42768	Florence No. 1	52.50

OUR HANDSOME $9.98 MARKER.

No. 42800 OUR $9.98 Price includes the Marker and Base complete with any lettering selected, as appears in the illustration, and the price is based on the actual cost of cutting the work out of the quarry with but our one small percentage of profit added. This stone is handsomely polished, has a beutiful surface, and as shown in the illustration, it is trimmed with tracing and beveling. **WE PAY THE FREIGHT.** Height, with base, 20 inches. Size of base, 16x8x6 inches. Marker, 12x12x4 inches.
No. 42800 Price $9.98
For more letters than shown in cut, add for sunk name letters 6c each; for date letters, 2½c each.

OUR FINE $13.75 MARKER.

No. 42808 AT $13.75 we furnish this Marker, made of the same beautiful Royal Blue Vermont Marble as our $9.98 marker shown above, but a larger size, being 22 inches high and 18 inches wide at the base. It is thicker, heavier, and of different style, shape and carving. It is furnished complete with the base and delivered at your nearest railroad station in good order for $13.75, with the same amount of lettering as shown in the cut, or only a few cents per letter extra for any number of letters you desire. **We pay the freight.** Height with base, 22 inches; size of base, 18x8x6; size of marker, 14x14x4.
No. 42808 .... $13.75
If more lettering than shown in cut is desired, see prices for extra lettering on No. 42800.

OUR RICH $13.76 MARKER.

No. 42812 THIS $13.76 Marker is the same size and of the same rich unfading Royal Blue Marble as our fine $13.75 marker, but of a different style of carving, tracing and shape. It is furnished complete with the base, lettered as desired and only costs you $13.76, with the same number of letters as shown in cut. We pay the freight. Height with base, 22 inches; size of base, 18x8x6; size of marker, 14x14x4.
No. 42812 Price $13.76
For more letters than shown in cut, add for sunk name letters 6c each; for date letters, 2½c each.

OUR SUPERIOR $14.98 TOMBSTONE.

No. 42816 AT $14.98 we offer this Royal Blue Marble Marker, made of the same rich, unfading Vermont marble as all the others, but measuring 24 inches high and 18 inches wide at base. Is thicker and of a heavy, dignified style, making a superior looking tombstone. **We pay the freight.** Height with base, 24 inches; size of base, 18x8x8; size of marker, 16x14x4.
No. 42816 Price $14.98

Used by permission.

Funeral Customs

By the time embalming was beginning to be accepted in rural North Georgia — around the 1930's — the undertaker usually went to the home to embalm the remains. Since there were no telephones, someone had to go to town to ask the undertaker to come out to the house where the death had occurred. The undertaker took with him a portable "cooling board," upon which to embalm the body. At first, his equipment was not electric, so a hand pump was used. After the remains had been embalmed and were ready for viewing, the cooling board was then used as the reposing couch. The head of the board was raised, and a velvet pillow was placed under the head of the deceased. A velvet drape, with a silk lining, covered the body. The drape was called a "pall," and from this, came the term "pallbearer" for the men who carried the pall as it was draped over the body. The board also had a skirt or ruffle around it.

After the casket selection had been made, the undertaker sometimes waited until the day of the funeral to take the casket to the home. The body was then placed into it before the funeral, which was either held at the deceased's home or in the community church. Most funeral services were held the day after the death occurred, at 11 o'clock in the morning.

The body of Preacher Farris is carried from his home enroute to his funeral and burial. He served as a Methodist Minister in White County. Claude (second from left) assisted in the service in 1945.

The funeral director would select the appropriate door wreath, which was normally made of crepe, and then attach it to, or near, the front door. When the majority of funerals were still being conducted from the home, floral wreaths took the place of the crepe. In rural areas, funeral directors carried artificial flower wreaths for the door with them.

Sometimes, older houses were not built to accommodate large objects being moved through the doorway. Often, doors had to be removed from their hinges, and in some cases, part of the framework, in order to get the coffin into the house. During the summer months, since homes and churches did not have screens on their windows and doors, a net cover would be placed over the casket when it was opened for viewing of the body.

Arranging seating, wording of the obituary, and transportation for relatives often could be a very sensitive thing. The funeral director had to have special skills in human relations to keep everyone satisfied. Likewise, the minister, too, had to possess skills in human relations; because then, as now, some of the relatives might not be on speaking terms with each other, or other family members making it necessary for the funeral director and the preacher to keep harmony among the participants.

A common arrangement of the procession was as follows: clergymen, honorary pallbearers, active pallbearers (when two groups were used), hearse, immediate family members, relatives, friends, and neighbors. If a fraternal order was to participate in the funeral service, it always took the lead. Before the automobile became a common means of transportation, the procession was made up of wagons. Whoever owned the best wagon in the community would often carry the coffin in his wagon. After automobiles began being used, all traffic on the roads and highways would pull to the side of the road and remain stopped until the procession had passed. This gesture was made as a sign of respect for the bereaved family. Because of the large numbers of automobiles today, and the speed at which most travel, a question of safety arises for continuing this practice. It is somewhat sad to think of losing this time-honored tradition.

At the cemetery, clergymen took the lead. The pallbearers deposited the coffin over the grave, and the preacher took his position, facing the family, and began the "Committal Service." The coffin was lowered into the grave either by pallbearers or by trained attendants. Filling the grave nearly always was done after the bereaved family members had left the cemetery. To some, however, remaining at the graveside until the casket was lowered into the ground aided in accepting the finality of losing the loved one.

Preparing for the committal service at Alta Vista Cemetery, Gainesville, GA, in 1948. Claude is standing at the far left.

By the middle of this century, the aesthetic appeal of the casket improved greatly by the use of soft toned colors. The use of floral arrangements as an expression of sympathy also increased. There have been many other changes in how people handle death, including one custom which has completely changed; the obituary in the local newspaper. The following is an obituary of the early 1900's, taken from the "History of Lumpkin County," as it appeared in a local newspaper:

DEATH OF MRS HENRY P. FARROW; from the **"Gainesville Eagle"** of August 18, 1904:
> The wife of our beloved Colonel Henry P. Farrow, postmaster of this city, died at her summer cottage at Porter Springs, Lumpkin County, Tuesday. Her husband and children, and most of her grandchildren, and her brother, Dr. Simpson of South Carolina, were at her bedside before she died. She was 68 years of age, and a native of South Carolina. She was a sister of former Governor Simpson of South Carolina. Her two daughters are Mrs. John A. Whitner and Mrs. John Cooper of Atlanta. Mrs. Farrow was a type of the finest Southern womanhood of which the aristocratic days of the antebellum times boasted — an earnest, sweet-spirited Christian, a domestic queen, gifted far above many women in mental qualities and intellectual attainments, and adorned with all the graces of true and refined Southern womanhood. Her departure has caused intense sorrow.

In the 1800's and until the 1940's, members of the community took time off from their work to help dig a grave for a neighbor. To pay someone to dig the grave would have been disgraceful. Some men took great pride in the knowledge and skills which they used in digging graves. To them, digging a grave was much more than just digging a hole in the ground; it was an art. There were no metal caskets or steel vaults, and the wooden coffin offered little protection from the elements. Thus, a properly dug grave could be a great comfort to the family.

The men would dig down to a certain width and set the wall in about four inches on each side. Oak planks were then placed on each side, so dirt never rested on the coffin. This was called a vault. Another option was to dig a ledge around the inside of the grave and set a grave arch on it. The arch looked like a corrugated piece of metal, and helped keep the grave from settling.

New Holland Mills, located on the outskirts of Gainesville, Georgia, had a crew of men who went to different communities and helped dig graves. They started doing this just for the employees at the mill and their families, but soon, they were helping others, too. Local funeral homes helped them by providing a truck to use for transportation so they could easily reach other communities.

When there was an emergency or help was needed in the community, the church bell would be rung, or someone would go door-to-door to mobilize the community to action. Today, the church bells no longer sound the call for help, and the modern community does not respond physically as a whole unit. The lack of acquaintance with neighbors and diversity of work schedules, combined with the hours and distances away from home each day, preclude the simple oneness of the earlier rural community, when nearly everyone made their livelihood in the same way.

Claude conducted the funeral service for a child of the Jarrard family of White County in 1939. Services were held at Mt. Pleasant Methodist Church.

Personal Reflections

Folks were fiercely proud and independent in the Georgia mountains at the turn of the century. They had all they could do to take care of their own family and did not really have time to get involved with their neighbors, unless there was a need. When help was needed, everyone helped as they could, because one never knew when they might need some assistance from a neighbor the next time. Growing up in this environment, Claude Hood learned to care about his fellowman. He always had an outgoing, caring personality, and after his call into the ministry, his empathy and great concern for the sick, dying, and bereaved were quickly visible to the communities he served. He also showed great kindness toward older members of his congregations. Special efforts were always made to visit in the homes, hospitals, and other institutions where people needed him.

Claude has answered many, many calls and requests. Family members have called him to come sit with, and pray for, the sick and dying in the middle of the night, as well as in the middle of the day. For those churches that he did not pastor he often ran revivals or preached there at one time or another, so most folks in and around the five counties where he pastored knew of him or knew him personally. So, for these reasons, he was called upon to help non-members as often as his members. He was a part of so many families. They were all his friends, and he cared deeply for them. "No" was always the most difficult word for him to use. Unless a previous commitment had already been made, he always went when and wherever he was asked to go.

He has always considered it an honor to be able to help, in some way, when called upon by those families who have lost a loved one. To most people, Claude Hood was not just their pastor; he was, and is today, their friend. Friends share with you, your pain and joys, and they can cry, laugh, and share treasured remembrances of a lost loved one. Claude did all these things, but of greatest importance, was his loving reminder to the families of God's love; not only for the deceased, but even more, for those who were left. His faith and belief in God's love for everyone were always lovingly and patiently demonstrated through his words and in his quiet, sincere prayers. Although he is not physically able to maintain the same pace today as in years past, when he does speak, his commanding presence in the pulpit, along with his comforting loving message of hope, are just as strong as they have ever been.

Claude (center) stands with other ministers at a funeral in 1945. Note the black net spread over the open casket. This was the custom during the years when the remains of the deceased were returned home after embalming until time for burial. There were few screens on windows and doors, and the net helped keep away flying insects when the casket was opened for viewing.

One of Claude's trademarks at funerals has always been his quoting passages of the Bible from memory. Some of his most frequently used are: The 23rd Psalm, "*The Lord is my shepherd; I shall not want...;*" St. John, chapter 14, verses 1 - 6, "*Let not your heart be troubled: ye believe in God, believe also in me...;*" II Corinthians, chapter 5, verse 1, "*For we know that if our earthly house of this tabernacle were dissolved, we have a building of God, an house not made with hands, eternal in the heavens;*" and Revelation, chapter 14, verse 13, "*And I heard a voice from heaven saying unto me, Write, Blessed are the dead which die in the Lord from henceforth: Yea, saith the Spirit, that they may rest from their labours; and their works do follow them.*" Although numerous interpretations of the Bible are available today, Claude preaches from the King James Version.

Like all other things, church music has changed over the years. Today, many funerals only use recorded instrumental music, but when there is vocal music, the songs are different as well. Some of the old hymns that were sung at funerals were: "*When They Ring the Golden Bells;*" "*What a Friend;*" "*Sweet By-and-By;*" "*Nearer My God to Thee;*" and Claude's favorite hymn, "*Amazing Grace.*"

During the researching and writing of this book, there have been numerous interviews, as well as correspondence, with Claude's friends and acquaintances. Some of these people have known him since he was a young minister, while others have known him only in the latter years. The large number of funerals that he has conducted over the years is frequently mentioned. Unfortunately, no exact records have been kept of the total number. There is no doubt, however, that he has spoken at thousands of funerals. There were many weeks that he had at least one funeral every day, and often, he conducted three services during the same day. He has always made an effort to visit with the family of the deceased, the day or night before the funeral, and to spend additional time with them again prior to the service on the day of the funeral.

Funeral Customs

The following are excerpts from interviews and correspondence about this part of Claude's ministry, as thoughts and feelings were expressed by his friends and acquaintances.

"You only bury your friends. Somebody else will bury the others. This is how Claude has worked with most of the funerals he's preached. Everytime you bury a friend, you bury a little bit of yourself. It takes a strong man to hold up under that much loss. Working with the bereaved never has gotten old to him, or too much for him to deal with. Sometimes I've seen him get very exhausted, physically.

"When he had trouble with his back, the doctor had put him to bed because he was in so much pain. He got out of bed and went to this funeral, and after he finished the committal service at the cemetery, he couldn't walk back to his car, so we had to take him out of the cemetery in the hearse. It was just hard for him to say "no" to somebody if they called him.

"There's lots in these parts that don't feel like they can bury their dead, unless Claude helps with the funeral.

"For generations, members of the families remember that he has shared all of their grief over the years. He's just the one they call when some of the family dies. He's always been there.

"Claude was always so compassionate with folks. He could certainly touch on the situation. If he had a suicide, Claude could handle it delicately. Everybody's not a saint. You can't preach 'em all into heaven, so sometimes he had to preach more to the folks attending than about the deceased.

"I never saw Claude meet a stranger. He could just walk up to a crowd, and before they knew it, he knew more about them than they realized. He could just mix with people. He had an outgoing personality; wasn't overbearing.

"One of his traits was to go around and shake the hands of the family and then with the pallbearers, after every funeral. He's always done that, and still does.

"The reason he's called to do so many funerals is because he has such a soothing affect on the families. He's so reverent, and he gives them confidence. He always seems to find something good to say about the biggest sinner. He may shed tears with the family, but he never delivers a sermon that gets them more emotional. He's very positive. He offers them reassurance and thoughts of themselves in dealing with their loss.

"When he starts quoting scripture, in his kind voice, there's no way you can be as sad as you were before he started. And he's said lots of times, 'If you're ready to meet God, a funeral should be a celebration of triumph.' He's really like the Good Shepherd; he cares about each sheep."

Claude's response to these statements, and to other compliments or gestures of appreciation for what he's done to help someone, a church, or a community is quick, from his heart, and always the same, "I haven't done anything; God has done it all."

There have been times in everyone's life, when it has been a definite struggle to work through a given problem. There is also the old saying that "a problem is only an opportunity in disguise." There were plenty of "opportunities" confronting the mountain folks, as they began to enjoy the convenience of travel from one place to another in an automobile. However, the mountain roads had not caught up with the progress of the automobile. During bad weather, the Georgia mountains' red clay presented many problems to the individuals trying to drive the automobile over the axle-deep, muddy roads. Looking back, some of these situations bring smiles today, but they were not very humorous then!

During his years in the ministry, Claude has worked with many funeral directors. However, struggles to overcome common problems presented by the elements, created lasting bonds of friendship between him and those with whom he worked so closely during those days of the thirties, forties, and fifties. One local funeral director laughingly tells of his first meeting with Claude:

"It was in 1946, during the cold month of February. We had a funeral service at Mt. View Baptist Church, in White County. The deceased had lived on Shoal Creek prior to his death, and it was his request that Claude and the Rev. Homer Thomas conduct his funeral.

"The weather had been bad, and the back roads, being dirt, with a little gravel here and there, were almost impassable. The ruts were knee-deep, and the cars were dragging the bottom as they came up this steep grade in the road. The body of the deceased had been at home and was being taken to the church for the funeral and for burial in the church cemetery. Mr. Homer was in the lead car, and Claude was behind him. I was behind Claude in the hearse.

"As we started up the hill, Mr. Homer met two sisters, who lived nearby, walking up the road. Being acquainted with them, he thought he would stop and offer them a ride, because the road was so muddy. So, he just pulled up and stopped right there on that hill, in the middle of the road. They had a short conversation, opened the door, knocked some of the mud off of their feet, and got into his car.

"Well now, of course, there was no way anybody was going anywhere on that road! We had to get out and push every car to get it started up that steep grade again! Needless to say, we were all covered with mud by the time we got through, but we went right on to the church and had the funeral."

* * * * *

In another story, he related that a man, who had lived up toward Kinsey Town at Goat Neck, above Cleveland, had died.

"The weather was real bad. It had been raining and sleeting, and they had been working on the roads up that way. The undertakers had gone in over the muddy roads to the man's house about 2 a.m. the morning before. They took the old gentleman's body to the funeral home for embalming.

"After we got to Cleveland, the family decided they wanted to take his body back home, so we finally got him back out to the house. The funeral was to be the next day at 11 o'clock in the morning. The day of the funeral, Claude rode with me, because I had chains on my tires. That morning, a man who worked for the county came and brought a tractor to help pull the hearse and other cars out. At about 2 o'clock in the afternoon, the procession finally made it to the main highway (the Cleveland and Helen Highway).

"At the highway, we stopped, and as I got under the car to remove the chains, this big blob of red mud, about the size of a trash can, fell on my chest and just covered me up in mud! Well, I knew Claude would get a good laugh out of this. It didn't matter to him that he was almost as muddy as I was. So, I yelled up to him: If you laugh, I'll get even with you if it's the last thing I ever do! We had a real good laugh over that mess. We might as well laugh, we couldn't get there any quicker, and there certainly wasn't a thing we could do about all that mud. So, we went right on to the little country church, and the crowd was still waiting for us, just like we were on time.

"Lots of times Claude had two or three funerals on the same day. He knew about how much time he had for each service and allowed pretty good travel time. But during the war, the soldiers' funerals were pretty hard. Usually, we knew all of them from the community, and when they came back in boxes, it hurt. Sometimes, the Army would send several at once. This made it harder on everybody. One time, at a church in White County, Claude was helping with a joint funeral for three local boys. It was really hard emotionally for the families and all of us. Claude knew he had to be at another service, but he just seemed to have more to say that day. He came down out of the pulpit, still preaching, and walked to the families and shook all of their hands, still talking as he went, he finally finished his sermon when he got to the side door of the church. We saw him running from the church to his little black car, jump in, and take off down that dirt road leaving a cloud of dust behind him.

"There is a story that has been told for years as the truth about a practical joke several young boys pulled on a man who lived in their community. It seems that this man had a reputation of going on drinking binges. During these times, he liked to walk through the community and could be found the day after the binge, wherever he had slept it off.

"The boys knew that man's behavior patterns pretty well. So on one particular night, they followed him on his way home, as he made his rounds through the community. As usual, he passed out before he got home. The boys also knew that there was to be a funeral at the church the next day. So being boys, they thought a practical joke would be fun. They carried the sleeping man to the cemetery and let him down into the open grave, leaving him to sleep the binge off. They thought it would be fun to wait around for him to wake up and see his reaction to finding himself in a grave. (There were no funeral home tents, blankets of grass, or anything else at the grave site during these years.) As the sun came up over the cemetery, they heard the poor old man moaning, as he began to come to. From their hiding place, they could see two hands emerge over the edge of the fresh dirt and slowly the rest of his body. He stood up, looked around, and assuming that he was alone in the cemetery, proudly announced, 'Well, resurrection morning, and the first one up!' He looked around and seemed to be expecting other graves to open; but after awhile, scratching his head and looking a bit confused, his expression seemed to say that some things are just beyond explanation! With a last glance back at "his" grave, he walked off down the road toward his house."

The Center Of Each Community

There is nothing quite as picturesque as the small, country churches that dot the hills and valleys of North Georgia. Their steeples reach skyward as a special symbol of reverence. The architecture of the buildings varies from the simple to the ornate, with each having its own distinctive appearance. And no matter what the season, their beauty is unsurpassed.

Claude E. Hood has been blessed by being able to experience the unique personalities of many of these lovely church buildings. Some have rich histories and were built by ancestors of long ago, while others being new, are just as interesting and exciting in their own way because of the sense of new life they seem to radiate. Being a part of each of these communities and church congregations for 55 years, has been most rewarding. He has seen much change with the passing of these many years. Not only have the church buildings changed with the times, but so have the people who attended them. Although the improvements and changes are intended to improve our quality of life, occasionally there is a fleeting lump in the throat and a tear in the eye as shadows of yesterday's joys remind us that they will be no more. The hardships and struggles become only a faint memory, as those emotions that were pleasant and enjoyable take over. Since the church was the center of life for each community, it met the spiritual, social, and often, the educational needs of the community.

This chapter contains a brief history of the 27 churches, in five counties, which Claude has pastored. During the 1800's and well into the 1900's it was common for rural churches to serve as the house of worship one Saturday and one Sunday of each month, and on weekdays the building was used as the community school. Because services were held only twice each month, many preachers were able to pastor more than one church at the same time. Most rural churches served small, local communities and memberships varied in number from church to church. Attendance could be considerably more or less depending upon the weather and if there was a special service at the church.

The business meeting of the church was held once each month, usually on Saturday afternoon (in later years, on Saturday night), before the regularly scheduled worship service on Sunday. Presently, churches have their business meetings on Sunday or Wednesday nights before the regularly scheduled Sunday morning or afternoon worship service. While each church had its own rules of conference, most were either the same or very similar. The church clerk was responsible for informing a new pastor of the church rules. One rule stated that no one could go out of the church building while conference was in session. If they did, they had to rise to their feet and ask the moderator to be excused, and the moderator would then grant or refuse their request. Another rule stated that women were not allowed to speak in conference. There are some churches that still enforce this rule today.

Early church pews or benches were made locally and consisted of one plank to sit on and one plank to lean back on. Sometimes slats were used instead of planks. The benches were very uncomfortable, and made it more difficult for some members to doze during the sermon.

Not all families observed the Sabbath Day (Sunday) in the same way. All businesses, such as stores, restaurants, gas stations, etc. were closed on Sunday. No work was done on Sunday unless there was an emergency which could not wait until Monday. Most families did prepare food and allowed the children to play games on Sunday; however, there were some who believed that Sunday should be a day of absolute rest. All food preparation was done on Saturday, and children could play no games on the Lord's Day.

An old church pew made of slats, taken from a Lumpkin County church.

In 1945-46 Claude was pastor of five churches, with one being full-time. Although Westside was a full-time church, he had an assistant pastor preach two Sunday mornings each month for him. Each Sunday and Wednesday night he was at Westside. At this time he and Edna lived on Brown's Bridge Road, in Gainesville, Georgia, and they drove to White County three Sunday afternoons and two Saturday afternoons each month for regular services.

Claude Hood's Church Schedule In 1945-46

1st Sunday - Dewberry Church # 1, Morning.
(Hall County)

2nd Sunday - Westside Church, Morning.
(Hall County)

2nd Sunday - Mt. View Church, Saturday and Sunday, Afternoon.
(White County)

3rd Sunday - Dewberry Church # 2, Morning.
(Hall County)

3rd Sunday - County Line Church, Saturday and Sunday, Afternoon.
(White County)

4th Sunday - Westside Church, Morning.
(Hall County)

4th Sunday - Mt. View Church, Afternoon.
(White County)

Note: Dewberry # 1 and Dewberry # 2 also had a monthly Saturday Conference service. Westside Church held its business session on Sunday night, once each month.

Many years ago someone gave Claude the following advice. They thought it was appropriate for him and held some basic truths which he should remember, as he hurried from one place to another over the roads of North Georgia:

Sing While You Drive

At 45 miles per hour sing...
"Highways are Happy Ways!"

At 55 miles per hour, sing...
"I'm but a stranger here!"

At 65 miles per hour, sing...
"Nearer My God to Thee!"

At 75 miles per hour, sing...
"When the Roll is Called
up Yonder, I'll be There!"

At 85 miles per hour, sing...
"Lord, I'm Coming Home!"

Claude Hood, 1940's

Since announcing his ministerial call 55 years ago, in 1932, Claude has pastored 27 Baptist churches in five northeast Georgia counties. Of these 27 churches, he has pastored six of them twice. Those pastored twice are: Amy's Creek Church, B. C. Grant Church, Dewberry Church # 2, Mt. Vernon Church, Tesnatee Church, and Center Grove Church, thus giving a total of 33 pastorates during his ministry. He pastored Mt. View Church in White County, his home church, for 29 consecutive years, longer than any other church.

As far as Claude knows he has never forgotten a scheduled service he was supposed to attend during the 55 years. He has seldom ever been late; then only due to circumstances beyond his control. The only times he has ever failed to keep an appointment to speak, he was confined to bed by his doctor. These times have been few indeed. All these years his motto seems to have been action because of commitments, not action or lack of action based upon how one feels. He never went on a family vacation at a time that would require him to miss a church service. Vacations were scheduled around his commitment to the church, and then if there was a call for help at the last minute, the car would be unpacked, and the vacation put on hold until another day.

In 1984, Claude resigned from Center Grove Church and has not pastored a church since; however, he continues to conduct numerous funerals and weddings and often visits the sick and shut-ins. He is also enjoying visiting and speaking at various churches throughout the area and remains busy with an active schedule despite his "retirement."

Amy's Creek Baptist Church

Alex Mountain Road
Clarkesville, GA

CONSTITUTED: 1834

PASTORED: Six years (pastored twice)
1933 - 1935 and 1936 - 1940
(approximate dates)

Amy's Creek began as a log structure on an old Indian trail — a road known as the Unicoi Turnpike — near Georgia Highway 17 about midway between Clarkesville and Helen. The original building also doubled as a school for some fifty years, before being replaced by a new framed building around 1890.

The present building was begun during the late 1930's and completed in 1941. Today's membership of 175 is proud to say that Amy's Creek is one of the oldest Baptist churches in Habersham County. Amy's Creek was the first church Claude pastored in Habersham County. Services were held on Saturday afternoon before the third Sunday and on the third Sunday morning. During his first pastorate Claude did not have a car, and the church was too far from his home to walk. So, one of the members who lived near Cleveland, would pick him up on the third Saturday and take him to church. The members of the church took turns, as was the custom, inviting the preacher to stay overnight in their home. Then, some of the members would take him to Sunday morning service and home in the afternoon. If he was needed for a funeral, they went to his home and got him. By the second time he was called to the church, he had bought a car.

One family, destined to impact Claude's life greatly in future years, attended Amy's Creek regularly during the first pastorate and frequently during his second pastorate. This was the Hubert Burke family. Hubert's wife, Lola, was a member of Amy's Creek. Their youngest daughter, Edna, at the age of 14, was converted and baptized by Claude during the second time he served the church. Little did he know that she would one day become his wife.

The church was also sometimes attended by former Governor of Georgia, Lamartine G. Hardman, who owned a home and property in nearby Nacoochee Valley, Habersham County. While pastor at Amy's Creek, Claude returned to school and graduated. In addition to Amy's Creek, he simultaneously pastored Mt. View, Crescent Hill, and Blue Creek.

Claude Hood
1930's

B. C. Grant Baptist Church

P. O. Box 456
Cornelia, GA

CONSTITUTED: 1894

PASTORED: Eleven years, (pastored twice)

1950 - 1959 and 1976 - 1978

In November, 1894, fifteen Christian people met one mile north of Alto, Georgia, in Habersham County, to organize a church. The building and two acres of property were donated by Thomas Jefferson Grant in honor and memory of his departed son Captain B. C. Grant, whose body was the first to be laid to rest in the new church cemetery. Thus, the church became known as B. C. Grant Baptist Church of Christ, later to be shortened to B. C. Grant Baptist Church.

In July, 1895 the church adopted the Rules of Decorum and appointed delegates to the Union Meeting. In September, 1895, they approved application for membership in the Liberty Baptist Association. The following are excerpts from the minutes as they were recorded over the years:

- *In 1897, communion was postponed from May to June, because no wine was purchased and a collection amounting to 29 cents was received for this purpose.*

- *July, 1897, was the first time Sabbath School was mentioned, and the church voted to give the School 20 cents of the church's money.*

- *April, 1898, a collection amounting to 15 cents for the purchase of communion wine was received.*

- *Around 1900, the church voted to meet on Saturday before the third Sunday and the third Sunday. In April, the church voted to move the meeting time from 11 a.m. to 2:30 p.m. on Saturday.*

- *In November, 1903, the church voted to let the people of the community build a public school house on church land.*

- *In March, 1905, a Sunday School was organized.*

- *In July, 1908, the church voted to have a committee look after the enlargement of the meeting house.*

- *In May, 1910, the church purchased a bell.*

- *In March, 1912, the church organized a Singing Society.*

- *In 1914, the church voted to petition the Home Mission Board of Atlanta to contribute to a local minister the amount that the Board saw fit.*

- *In July of 1914, the church voted to take up a subscription to have the well dug for the school and church use.*

- *April, 1917, saw the church adopt a resolution to organize a Board of Deacons and Laymen.*
- *In February, 1924, the church voted to build an Odd Fellows hall over the school house.*
- *July, 1929, the church agreed to meet on Thursday and Friday to clean off the cemetery.*
- *In November, 1933, the church made up a shipment of farm products to ship to the Baptist Children's Home. To pay the freight, the church took up a collection.*
- *In April, 1938, the church voted to light the church with electric lights, by signing up with the R.E.A. in August. That same month, Alfred L. Gailey was elected as chairman of the Board of Deacons. Ordained in 1911, Gailey also served as the church clerk from September, 1907, until September, 1928, giving 21 years of continuous service.*
- *The church voted in October of 1942, to send the boys from B. C. Grant Community serving in the armed forces a Testament. In November, the church sent to the Orphans' Home $9.00 received in offering.*
- *In May of 1943, the church sent Georgia Baptist Hospital $22.10.*
- *The church voted in November of 1945, to build a new building with four class rooms. Completed in 1947, the church then voted to have two services each month, on the first and third Sundays.*
- *In 1949, the church voted to move the time for Saturday Conference to the third Saturday night.*
- *During 1951, plans were underway to install a heating system and baptismal pool.*

Rev. and Mrs. Willis Pruitt. Rev. Pruitt pastored East Side Baptist Church, Athens, GA, and often helped Claude in revivals.

In 1957, while Claude was pastor, the membership voted to build eight new classrooms and to brick the building's exterior. When some members questioned whether the church could afford the expansion, Claude expressed the opinion that he didn't think they could afford not to grow with the community. He said, "I've never heard of a church building being sold for its debts!" The improvements were made and paid for, and in 1959, the church voted to go full-time. Claude resigned during his second ministry at B. C. Grant due to poor health from injuries sustained in an automobile accident, which occurred while he was visiting shut-in members in the church community. The church has continued to make improvements and today is a source of strength for the community it serves.

Habersham Baptist Church

P. O. Box 412
Habersham, GA

CONSTITUTED: 1909

PASTORED: Three years, 1942 - 1945

A Presbytery made up of 16 men from Amy's Creek and Fairfield Baptist Churches met in 1909, to organize the Habersham Baptist Church. A church house built in the Habersham Mills Village served the Baptists and Methodists alike, until the early 1920's, when both groups moved to Habersham Mills School, where more room was available for worship service and Sunday School. The Baptist group had services two Sundays each month, and the Methodists had services two Sundays each month. Officers of the Church alternated each year, having a Sunday School Superintendent from the Baptists one year and from the Methodists the next year. Both groups worked well together, and attendance was good.

The Church continued to grow over the years, and on October 14, 1944, while Claude was the pastor of Habersham, it was voted to build a new Baptist church. A primary consideration in this decision was to enable Habersham Baptist Church to belong to the Baptist Association. Following the vote, a building fund was begun, with Claude leading the members in getting pledges so the new church could become a reality and better serve the community. The present structure, completed in 1948, was built on land donated by Habersham Mills. The Church has continued to grow and serve the community, and today it has a membership of approximately 400.

When Claude was called to Habersham Baptist Church, very few roads in rural counties and towns were paved. The main road from Cleveland to Clarkesville was still a dirt road, and sometimes in bad weather the roads would be so muddy that the cars could hardly drag through the ruts. Claude was single when he was called to Habersham in 1942, but married while he was pastor of the church.

Nacoochee Baptist Church

Sautee, GA

CONSTITUTED: 1850

PASTORED: Two years, 1953 -1955

Nacoochee Valley has a very important place in the history of Habersham and White Counties. Nacoochee Baptist Church is also a part of that history. Excerpts from the minutes during the 1800's read as follows:

- *Delegates were elected to the Clarkesville Association in 1888.*

- *On January 5, 1889, the church met in conference. Called for fellowship — not found in peace. Moved and seconded to bring a charge against a sister for falsehood. Moved and seconded also to bring a charge against a brother for shooting in a shooting match.*

- *On February 4, 1833, resolution passed by Nacoochee Church: Resolved that we the Church of Christ at Nacoochee while in conference have decided that it is unscriptural and therefore wrong for members of the Church to attend these settlement plays often called candy pullings and various other names. Resolved further that we will deal with our members as the Scripture directs for attending these plays or for playing at any time. Done in conference, February 4, 1893. Signed, Moderator and Church Clerk. (Plays or playing was another way of saying dances or dancing, at that time.)*

Like other churches of the time, the membership book listed males and females separately. In 1954, the report to the Habersham County Association showed a church memberhship of 175. Although it had a very small budget, the church did give the Orphans' Home (Georgia Baptist Children's Home) food and money that year. As the community around the Nacoochee Baptist Church has grown in recent years, so has the church.

Dewberry Baptist Church No. 1

Clarkes Bridge Road
Gainesville, GA

PASTORED: Nine years, 1940 - 1949 (estimated)

Dewberry Baptist Church No. 2

Cleveland Road, Highway 129
Gainesville, GA

PASTORED: Nine years, (pastored twice)
1942 - 1946 and 1961 - 1966

Both Dewberry Baptist Church No. 1 and Dewberry Baptist Church No. 2 share the same origin of constitution in 1821. The original church was one of nine Baptist churches constituting the Chattahoochee Baptist Association in 1826. Following the split in the original church, it is said that the membership of the group who moved to Clarkes Bridge Road remained in the Chattahoochee Baptist Association.

The group in the church on the Cleveland Road, Highway 129, remained in the original building and did not attend the Association until years later. When application was made and acceptance granted for membership in the Association, the Cleveland Road Dewberry Baptist Church was admitted as Dewberry Baptist Church No. 2. The two churches have been so distinguished as No. 1 and No. 2 since then. Claude is said to have been the only pastor to serve both Dewberry churches at the same time.

The following is an article taken from THE TIMES, Gainesville, Georgia, Sunday, April 23, 1978. The article was written by Sybil McRay, a recognized historian on the development of Hall County and the Baptist Denomination:

> Three years after the creation of Hall County, the Dewberry Baptist Church was established. Nineteen years later, there was a division. Then, there were two Dewberry Baptist churches. They added the Roman numerals I and II for identification. The story of the split in the congregation has been told throughout the years: "Hungry dog breaks up Church."

The Dewberry Baptist Church was established April 21, 1821, with 12 members. W. H. Craig, editor of a Gainesville paper, wrote the story of the split of the Dewberry Church, which was published in the ATLANTA JOURNAL, in 1929:

'*In the northern part of Hall County, in Tom Bell district, is a small Baptist church known as Dewberry No. 1. About two miles away, in Quillian's district, stands Dewberry No. 2, another Baptist church.*

Midway between them, Little River lends an impartial hand to both in their baptismal rites and then goes on its way through pastoral scenes to join up with the Chattahoochee.

In the year 1821, a little band of Baptist brethren got together, organized, and erected a small church building and named it Dewberry. When the Chattahoochee Baptist Association was organized at Hopewell Church in 1826, Dewberry was one of the charter members, represented by Rev. James Ryley and Henry Dobson who reported twenty-three members.

The church flourished as a "tree planted by the waters." Leading members of the congregation were Philip Byrd and George Chapman. Chapman had come to the community in 1831, from South Carolina with a large family of children. Byrd was native-born and childless, but with an adopted daughter.

Brother Byrd was a man of pronounced opinions, especially on theology, and obstinate and irascible disposition. "Argufying" was his natural element, and he defended his views vigorously and against all comers. He and Brother Chapman were constant contenders in the arena of religious disputation. Brother Byrd held firmly to the doctrine of Election and Reprobation — that God had from the beginning ordained that certain individuals should be saved for a life of future bliss and others irretrievably lost, and that without any strings or provisos to it.

Brother Chapman wasn't so certain. He would often say to Brother Byrd in his quiet way during their many arguments that it didn't look to him like fair play for the Deity to send a soul into the world with a mortgage already on it that never matured and couldn't be paid off. To which Brother Byrd would respond, often heatedly, that it didn't matter a straw how it looked to him, it was taught by St. Paul in his epistles.

And thus, they had it, nip and tuck, and these old fathers would argue in bootless discussions on theology. Out of these discussions and the rancor engendered by them a storm-child was born. Another Dewberry came into being.

A difference of sentiment had arisen among the brethren in regard to calling a pastor. Brother Byrd wanted Rev. Thomas Kimsey, while Brother Chapman favored Rev. Jackie Rives. Their followers divided into two camps, and somewhat strained relations ensued.

A spark was furnished one fateful day to set off the tinder that was dry. The two belligerent old brethren were dining together, and the endless and futile argument was again taken up. Brother Byrd, as usual, by reason of his ready tongue and agressiveness, had Brother Chapman about faded, and with an exultant glance at the enemy, he stabbed his fork into a choice piece of fried chicken, waved it aloft, and exclaimed, "Brother Chapman, it was predestinated before the foundation of the world that I was to eat this piece of chicken!" A sudden inspiration seized Brother Chapman that he might be the humble instrument in disproving the whole theory of fixed destinies. So as quick as a flash he seized a biscuit and pulled down on that piece of chicken, hitting it amidships.

A gloomy, flop-eared dog was near the men just waiting for someone to throw a morsel in his direction. He smelled the delectable morsel as it swished through the air and made such a catch as would do credit to a big league infielder.'

The Center Of Each Community 157

This incident caused a split in the church. Chapman and his followers seceded. All but three of the seventy-five members pulled out and went to Old Red Stick, an old and abandoned Methodist church not very far away. Here they met together until they could build a new house of worship.

Brother Byrd gathered his three faithful ones under his wing, got a preacher to come once a month, and went ahead. He kept the church records and the more the opposition asked for them, the more he clung to them. As the years went by, the membership grew little by little. It was an independent church, sufficient unto itself, owing no allegiance to anybody or anything, except the Lord.

In 1867, twenty-seven years after the division, and Brother Byrd having passed to his death, Rev. Joseph Chapman was called to the pastorate. He was a son of George Chapman and had married the adopted daughter of Philip Byrd. Pastor Chapman induced the membership to seek admission to the Chattahoochee Association.

The church now known as Dewberry No. 1 is the one established in 1840, by Chapman and his followers, while the church where Byrd remained as a member is now Dewberry No. 2. The designation being fixed by the date at which each joined the Association.

* * * * *

CARD GRADE AUGUST 10, 1924

Lesson Text: John 2: 1-11

TOT LESSON.

THE FIRST MIRACLE OF JESUS

MOTTO TEXT: Whatsoever he saith unto you, do it. John 2: 5.

1. Where was Jesus' mother? Answer—At a marriage in Cana of Galilee. 2. Who was invited to this marriage, also? Answer—Jesus and His disciples. 3. What did they need? Answer—Wine. 4. Who told Jesus that they had no wine? Answer —His mother. 5. What did Jesus' mother tell the servants to do? Answer—Just what Jesus said to do. 6. What was set before Jesus? Answer—Six water-pots of stone. 7. What did Jesus say to do? Answer—Fill the water-pots with water. 8. When they had done this what did Jesus say? Answer— "Draw it out and carry it to the governor of the feast." 9. What did they discover? Answer—That the water was turned to wine. 10. Of what was this the beginning? Answer—Of miracles performed by Jesus.

Published quarterly, in weekly parts, by the Baptist Sunday School Committee, Texarkana, Tex. Price, 5c. a quarter. Entered as second-class matter at post-office, Texarkana, Ark.-Tex. under the act of March 3, 1879. Printed in U. S. A.

Grade cards were given to children as their Sunday School Literature. A child might take a penny on Sunday to give to their Sunday School teacher to help pay for the cards.

Enon Baptist Church

P. O. Box 169
Lula, GA

CONSTITUTED: 1842

PASTORED: Two years, 1966 - 1968

The name of Enon Baptist Church is said to have been taken from the passage in the Bible, John 3:23. The original structure was torn down, and the congregation moved into the present building, which is now approximately 100 years old. Several years ago, this building was moved on the property to allow for construction of a highway and railroad.

During the 1960's, Enon's Sunday School saw steady growth, and during the years Claude served as pastor new Sunday School rooms and restrooms were added to the church. Additionally, an annual, week-long Winter Bible Study was begun. In 1967, Claude's wife Edna — serving as the Director — led the church in its first Vacation Bible School. Enon's membership now exceeds 200. Over the years, the church belonged to the Enon Baptist Association as part of the Georgia Baptist Convention. Presently, plans are underway to build a new church in the near future.

Fifth Sunday Youth Service at Enon Church on September 25, 1985. Front row (l-r) Claude, Rev. Loy Martin, Rev. Emmett Dale, and Rev. Lloyd Free. Back row (l-r) Rev. Luther Williams, Rev. Wayne Strickland, and Rev. Minor Martin.

Holly Springs Baptist Church

Route 1
Clermont, GA

CONSTITUTED: 1826

PASTORED: Nine years, 1947 - 1956 (estimated)

It is said that Holly Springs Baptist Church, as one of the older churches in Hall County, was given its name because of a large holly tree that branched out over a spring. The tree was located near what is now Highway 283. The original building was destroyed by a tornado in 1924, and the present building is the second structure to be built. It is now brick and completely remodeled inside.

During Claude's pastorate at the church, many changes were taking place in the area and in the way members of the church and the community earned their livelihood. The face of the community was changing from the family farm lifestyle to more diversified ways of making a living. This different lifestyle would eventually impact the church's influence on the surrounding community. Summer revivals were still very important to the rural way of life, however. Great meetings and crowds would attend, including not only the local folks but people from surrounding communities, too. At the end of the revival of 1948, thirty-eight converts were baptized, many of whom were adults. In 1952, the church was led in the largest Vacation Bible School in its history by Edna Hood, as principal. The church belonged to the Chattahoochee Baptist Association.

On June 29, 1986, led by Pastor Rev. Bill Lawson, the Holly Springs membership honored Claude and Edna for their work in the community over the years. As part of the tribute, a plaque, a love offering, and nine red roses — one for each of the years they served at the church — were given to them.

Rev. Bill Lawson (left), presenting plaque to Claude on Appreciation Day at Holly Springs Church, 1986.

Hopewell Baptist Church

Gainesville, GA

CONSTITUTED: 1808

PASTORED: 1955 - 1956

In 1808, when Hopewell Baptist Church was organized, the United States was only thirty-two years old, and it would be thirty- seven more years before the Southern Baptist Convention would be organized in 1845. Like many other churches in the early years, Hopewell also served as a school during the week. In the early 1800's there were few churches or schools in the area. The original building was a log structure with dirt floors. Several years later, it was replaced with a new building, and in 1889, the present building was begun. All three church buildings have been located on the same plot of ground.

In 1826, the Chattahoochee Baptist Association was organized at Hopewell. For many years prior to the Civil War, Negro slaves held membership in Hopewell Baptist Church and other churches in North Georgia. As members, they had a vote in the decisions of the church, but they could be counted on to vote as their owners did. Even after the Civil War, memberships were not moved from some churches for several years.

The church held two services each month on Saturday and Sunday until 1950, when it went half-time. Presently, Hopewell Baptist Church is a full-time church.

* * * * *

New Bridge Baptist Church Junior Sunday School Class taught by Edna Hood in 1968.

Mt. Vernon Baptist Church

Mt. Vernon Road, Route 9, Box 381
Gainesville, GA

CONSTITUTED: 1876

PASTORED: Eleven years (pastored twice)
1941 - 1944 and 1945 - 1953

Located on Mt. Vernon Road, just north of North Hall High School, Mt. Vernon Baptist Church was formed with 21 members and two deacons. The property on which to build the church was donated by John H. Odell. Mt. Vernon Baptist Church was accepted as a member of the Chattahoochee Baptist Association in 1880.

By 1883, the church membership had grown to 59. In 1887, with the membership having reached 69, letters of dismission were requested by 35 members asking to leave the church. In 1889, the church gave 16 cents to help finance the Baptist Association. By 1894, the church had 53 members and paid the pastor $35.00 as a salary for the year. In 1901, with a membership of 92, the church also paid the pastor $35.00 as the year's salary. Today's membership totals 420.

Rev. Will Nix (left) with Claude during the 1940's, at Mt. Vernon Church.

Over the years, the post office address of the church has changed numerous times. The church's address was not the only thing that changed through the years. The time of day for the Saturday Conference and Sunday Worship Services also changed several times, from afternoon to morning. Music was provided by a pump organ, and "fa-sol-la" singing was done from "The Sacred Harp" song book. The original church building was sold, when the present building was completed, in 1919. The church was lit by kerosene lamps, and one or two members of the church were appointed to be responsible for lighting the lamps for each service. During 1945, the church paid the pastor $431.70 as his salary for the year.

Rev. and Mrs. Scroggs Rogers.

Mt. Vernon Baptist Church was the first church Claude Hood pastored in Hall County. He was single when he was called to the church. He would drive down to the church for Conference on Saturday, and someone would invite him to spend Saturday night in their home, so he would not have to drive to White County and then right back the next day for the Sunday service. Claude always visited the sick and shut-ins in the community.

Several improvements were made to the church while Claude was pastor. He always had great pride in the churches he pastored — both in the church building and in the grounds — as well as in the people who made up the church body and the community it served.

New Bridge Baptist Church

Cleveland Road, Highway 129
Gainesville, GA

CONSTITUTED: 1879

PASTORED: Eleven years, 1961 - 1972

Ten charter members of New Bridge Baptist Church met in August of 1879, to officially form the new church. The property on which the church building stands was donated by Mary Chapman Whelchel, wife of Major Davis Whelchel. The church property was located on New Bridge Road, one of the main roads leading out of Gainesville at the time. Mrs. Whelchel further aided the church by requesting the donation of enough lumber to build the original church building. As a result of her request, Governor A. Chandler, who owned a sawmill at the time, graciously donated the necessary lumber for the construction.

The first church building was wood frame, with wooden benches made of slats. During the winter months, heat was provided by a four-legged, potbellied stove. Light was provided by oil lamps, and water was carried from a spring located near the church. The pastor received one pair of socks, knitted by Mrs. Whelchel, as payment for his services during the first year. Later, as the church grew and became more established, the pastor's salary ranged from $4.00 to $40.00, depending upon the success of that year's crops.

Sunday School was organized in 1884. The first song books contained no notes, only poetry. Later, the church would host many all-day convention singings, which included the singing of shaped notes. This type music was referred to as "fa-sol-la." The tradition of teaching music during singing schools was part of New Bridge's heritage, as well as most other rural churches during the early to mid 1900's. Sidney Lanier, famous singer and poet of the South, influenced many singers of the time. Lanier once wrote, "Music means Harmony, Harmony means Love, and Love means God." The children of the church raised enough money to buy the first musical instrument, an organ, costing $35.00.

Every summer, the church would have a week of "protracted meeting." The church yards and cemetery would be "cleaned off," and the trees in the groves were whitewashed. The baptizings would usually be held at Bell's Mill (originally Whelchel's Mill); but later, they were moved to the Chattahoochee River, then to the church pool, or to Lake Lanier.

Westside Baptist Church

1749 Atlanta Highway
Gainesville, GA

CONSTITUTED: 1939

PASTORED: Four years, 1946 - 1950 (estimated)

In 1939, at a tent revival being held on Hazel Street in Gainesville, a group of approximately 21 men and women realized they all had something in common. They wanted to see God's word carried to the people in their neighborhood. In an effort to make this a reality, they rented an old building on Lyman Street. The church was named Westside, because it was located on the west side of Gainesville.

To make the building more comfortable, they sealed it with brown paper to try to keep the cold out and the heat in. They partitioned-off Sunday School rooms with curtains. The early church was ministered to by an evangelist, but he was away often, and the congregation had to find a minister to "fill-in" for him.

Eventually, the group gave up the rented building and began holding services in the homes of individual members. They soon bought the property upon which the present building stands, and with everyone contributing what they could, a church was built on the site. By this time, pastors were called to serve the church congregation. Membership continued to grow, and in 1959, the original church building was torn down, and the present structure was built. Over the years, the church has continued to grow in the service of God. Today, the membership is approximately 457.

Claude was the fifth pastor at Westside. It was the first church to call him on a full-time basis, although he served five quarter-time churches at the same time. He preached at Westside two Sunday mornings each month, every Sunday night, and also attended Wednesday night prayer services. Westside was the first church Claude had pastored that had Sunday night services.

Westside was the first church to pay Claude a salary. All of the other churches he had pastored, and many after, paid whatever was collected when the hat was passed. During summer revivals, someone would sometimes be appointed to go into the community to "take-up" money for the preacher.

Claude had always helped support his family by growing most of their food, so instead of living in the parsonage he asked the church if they would rent a house for him with enough land to have a garden. They agreed and rented a house and sufficient property for a garden. This property was located on Brown's Bridge Road and rented for $25.00 per month. At this time, Claude's salary was $75.00 per month.

Pleasant Grove Baptist Church

Route 16
Gainesville, GA

CONSTITUTED: 1872

PASTORED: Four years, 1972 - 1976

In 1872, a group of men and women saw a need for a church in their community. Thirty in number, the charter members erected the first building, which was made of logs. Over the years, their membership has grown to approximately 370. In later years, the membership was able to construct a wooden building, and in 1957, a building fund was started to build a new church. On March 10, 1968, the present building was dedicated. Then, in 1971, the church began full-time services.

During Claude's pastorate at Pleasant Grove, his grandson Craig was converted, joined the church, and was baptized on April 25, 1976. Although Pleasant Grove Baptist Church has a Gainesville mailing address, it is located in Forsyth County near the Hall/Forsyth County lines.

* * * * *

Members of Pleasant Grove Baptist Church who attended the Appreciation Day Celebration for Claude in 1986, were (l-r): Claude, Mrs. Ray Hemphill, Mrs. Dewey Mathis, Mr. and Mrs. Duran, Mrs. Martin, Mr. and Mrs. Wood, and Edna.

Pleasant Grove Baptist Church Sunday School Class Members

1976

The Center Of Each Community 167

Vacation Bible Schools

Vacation Bible School Beginners' Class at Mt. View in 1952. Claudette second from left.

VBS a New Bridge Church, 1972. Claude's grandson Craig (r), Shelia Thomas, and Sherrie Hulsey (l).

Holly Spring Vacation Bible School in 1952, with Edna Hood, Director. Over 200 children were enrolled in the school.

Macedonia Baptist Church

Porter Springs Road, Route 1
Dahlonega, GA

CONSTITUTED: 1800's

PASTORED: Two years, 1935 - 1937

Fire destroyed the first church building; however, another was built which served its membership well for several years. It was eventually torn down and replaced with the structure in use today. It is thought that the church received its name from the Biblical name "Macedonia."

Claude was twenty-six when he was called to Macedonia. It was his first church in Lumpkin County. The church was located approximately ten miles from his home in the Mt. View Community of White County. He did not own a car at the time he was called, and his only way to get where he needed to be was to walk. He had discussed the distance before accepting the church, since Macedonia's Sunday service was at 11 a.m. and he had to be at Mt. View on the same Sunday afternoon by 2 p.m. It was felt by those to whom he talked, that he could walk the distance and make Mt. View's service without being late.

As a boy, Claude had learned the woods around his home in White County, but he was not as familiar with the back woods of Lumpkin County. He was given directions for going to Macedonia through the woods. He was told to cross the river at the Grindle Ford. (A ford is a shallow place in a creek or river that is used by wagons and people to get safely from one side to the other. Usually there is a footlog for the walker to use.) On his way to conduct his first service, Claude realized that he was lost and had to stop and get directions to the ford. Upon arrival, he found the footlog washed away. There was nothing to do but remove his shoes and socks, roll up his "breeches" and wade across. The story from this point on has two versions: the one passed down through several generations at Macedonia and other churches; and the one Claude tells.

The old timers said, "Claude took off his socks and put them in his pocket. In his hurry...because he was late to church...he forgot about them until about halfway through his sermon. He felt the need to wipe his brow, reached into his pocket for his handkerchief, and pulled out a sock instead."

Claude says he took off his socks to wade the river, and when he got to the other bank, it was sandy, and since his feet were wet, he couldn't put his socks on right then. He knew how late he already was, and getting to the church was his first concern. So, he ran the rest of the way to the church, putting his shoes on when his feet were dry. He remembers feeling embarrassed once inside the church, that the members would think he didn't have any socks to wear in October. It is a story that has brought many smiles to the faces of the tellers and the listeners alike.

The Center Of Each Community

When that first service was over at Macedonia, he realized that he would have to make very good time to get to Mt. View for the afternoon services. Members of Macedonia took turns loaning Claude a horse or a mule to ride to the river, thus cutting down on his travel time. At the ford, he would send the animal back home. From there, he would trot the rest of the way. Try as he might he was usually late getting to Mt. View, and part of his congregation would have gone home. However, the scheduled service was always held with those who were still waiting. Claude knew that somehow he would have to get a car. Eventually, he borrowed $500 and bought his first car. Another first in Claude's life also came while pastoring at Macedonia — his first wedding ceremony was performed there.

Presently, Macedonia's membership is 148. Over the years, the church has belonged to the New Union Baptist Association.

* * * * *

```
Vol. XXXIV          THIRD QUARTER, 1920          Number 3
                 PRICE: 4½ CENTS THE QUARTER


                                              July
        Senior                                August
                                              September
        Quarterly


        SOUTHERN BAPTIST CONVENTION SERIES
                    E. C. DARGAN, D.D., EDITOR


             Praise waiteth for thee, O God, in
             Zion; and unto thee shall the vow
             be performed. O thou that hearest
             prayer, unto thee shall all flesh come.
                              —Psalm 65:1, 2.


    Published Quarterly by the Sunday School Board of the Southern Baptist Convention
    161 Eighth Ave., North, Nashville, Tenn.  I. J. Van Ness, D.D., Corresponding Secretary
    ENTERED AS SECOND-CLASS MATTER AT THE POSTOFFICE AT NASHVILLE, TENNESSEE, UNDER ACT OF MARCH 3, 1879
```

At left is a copy of the cover of an adult Sunday School Quarterly belonging to Edna's mother. She used it in 1920.

Paid advertising was used inside the book. There were advertisements for furniture, clothing and the Edison Amberola phonograph and records.

Mt. Zion Baptist Church

Route 1
Murrayville, GA

CONSTITUTED: 1889

PASTORED: Two years, 1936 - 1938

Today Mt. Zion has a membership of approximately 225, and although the present structure is not the original, it has given many years of faithful service to the Mt. Zion Community. It is the same building that was in use when Claude was pastor in 1936. The design is very unique and one of the more picturesque church buildings in the area.

In order to accept the call of Mt. Zion, Claude had to resign as pastor of Macedonia Baptist Church. Many friendships were formed during those young years of his ministry, and they have proven to be sources of encouragement and support over the years.

Claude Hood in 1938.

Bethel Baptist Church

Cleveland, GA

CONSTITUTED: 1900

PASTORED: Two years, (mid to late 1930's; exact date not available)

Bethel was sometimes called Hickory Nut because the church services were held in the Hickory Nut School House before the actual church was built. The charter members of Bethel were originally members of Union Baptist Church. While Claude was pastoring Bethel, he also pastored five other churches.

The church belonged to the White County Association. Today Bethel has over 100 members.

* * * * *

Rev's. Forrester, Farrell Presley, Jack Pierce, Claude, Bill Lawson, and Winfred Durand at the Appreciation Day given by Holly Springs Church in 1986.

Blue Creek Baptist Church

Route 4
Cleveland, GA

CONSTITUTED: 1828

PASTORED: Seven years, 1934 - 1940

Blue Creek Baptist Church is one of the oldest churches in White County. It is located on State Highway 255. The original church was known as Sardis Baptist Church. The church building known as Sardis was located about 250 yards to the west of the present Blue Creek Church. A second site was located between the present site and the highway. The third church building was situated between the above locations (this is the church pictured). It burned on October 27, 1973. The present church building was built near the site of the second church. Being located in the Blue Creek Community, the church came to be called Blue Creek Baptist Church. The community also shares its name with the stream, which was life-giving to the early farmers living along its banks.

Claude was young and inexperienced when he was called to Blue Creek. He was not familiar with that area of White County. In today's mobile world that sounds strange; but, in the days when people had to walk or ride in a wagon everywhere they went travel was limited. Also, there was never time to travel far from home when farming was the only livelihood.

By this time, Claude had his first car to drive instead of walking to his churches. During those days of the depression, money was very hard to come by! When an offering was taken Claude might be given ten cents or less, and sometimes an offering was not even taken. Even in the early years, he established his well-known pattern of visiting the sick and shut-in members of the community, and this took gas. Many times he didn't have enough money to buy gas, but God always provided for his needs. Whenever it was possible, a deacon would accompany him on his visits throughout the community.

Blue Creek Baptist Church continues to prosper and presently has approximately 200 members. Over the years, it has been a member of the White County Baptist Association.

Claude Hood
1930's

Center Grove Baptist Church

Cleveland, GA

CONSTITUTED: 1912

PASTORED: Twelve years (pastored twice)
1955 - 1961 and 1978 - 1984

Recently, the church records were destroyed in a fire; therefore, there is no way to confirm much of the church history. There were fifty-two charter members who met to organize Center Grove Baptist Church.

On July 4, 1977, vandals set fire to the church, causing extensive damage to the sanctuary and its contents. Much of the original building was salvaged however, and rebuilt as it appears today. The present membership stands at approximately 80 members.

In 1932, the summer Claude announced his call to the ministry, he was the visiting minister at five revivals. The majority of these were working with Rev. Homer Thomas. Rev. Thomas pastored Center Grove at that time, and Claude's second week of revival was at Center Grove. The church overflowed at each service during the week, and there were over forty souls saved that week. All of the surrounding communities became involved in the revival, including Mossy Creek Methodist Church, just a short distance away. Claude's mother grew up at Mossy Creek, and her family still lived there, as did his grandparents, who also attended the revival. People came in wagons or walked to church that summer.

Despite the physical and emotional demands of that summer, it was a joyful one. There were times, however, that he felt he had made a complete flop. As a young man who had never stood before a congregation to speak or deliver a sermon, he felt inadequate in his knowledge of the Bible and his ability to deliver a sermon. There were times when he felt that the older, more experienced preachers could have done a better job in the pulpit; yet, Claude knew they could not deliver the message that God had given him. So he studied, prayed, and trusted in God's leadership to guide him then, as he still does today. Like anyone beginning a new career, he needed to be taught the ropes, so to speak, and this is just the role that Rev. Homer Thomas filled. He guided, led, pushed, encouraged, and believed in Claude. He supported him in his first steps. Over the years, Claude has referred to him as his "Father in the Work."

In honor of his 50 years of dedicated ministry Claude is presented with a gold watch by J. C. Rogers, representing the members of Center Grove Church.

Chattahoochee Baptist Church

Route 4
Cleveland, GA

CONSTITUTED: 1884

PASTORED: Three years, 1939 - 1942

On November 9, 1884, deacons from Blue Creek and Fairfield Baptist churches met for the purpose of organizing and building Chattahoochee Baptist Church. Some 73 years later, in 1957, a new building was begun to replace the original structure. It was completed in 1958. The present membership of Chattahoochee is 250. The church shares its name with the famous Chattahoochee River, which flows nearby. The church has belonged to the Mountain, Enon, and Chestatee Baptist Associations. The following are excerpts from some of the early church minutes:

- *December 13, 1884, took up a collection for a church book. Received 20 cents. The book cost 60 cents.*

- *March 14, 1885, met in Conference, called for peace and fellowship, invited visitors to sit in council, and called for reasons of absence of members.*

- *June 21, 1885, appointed delegates to the Mountain Association.*

- *July 18, 1885, took up collection for the Association Minutes; received 50 cents.*

- *September 19, 1885, charged member for living in adultery.*

- *October 17, 1885, excluded same member for living in adultery.*

- *September 18, 1886, took up collection for the church house and received $16.50 by subscription.*

- *November 20, 1886, liberated a member to speak in public.*

- *July 16, 1887, excluded a member for heresy and took up a collection for the minister.*

- *May, 1888, appointed a committee to talk with a member for indulging in intoxicating liquor.*

- *April, 1889, took up a collection for wine (wine used in communion).*

- *July, 1889, charges taken against a member for selling whiskey.*

- *August, 1891, passed a resolution to call the roll of male members at each conference and mark absentees. Absentees to give a reason for their absences; on failing to do so, the church would appoint a committee to see them.*

- *1902, a brother member and his wife were not in fellowship. Church withdrew fellowship from the members.*

- *January, 1903, elected member as Superintendent of the Sabbath School.*
- *December, 1903, no Conference because of bad weather.*
- *1909, church requested delegates to the Mountain Association to call for a letter of dismission from the Association.*
- *1910, church agreed to join the Enon Association.*
- *1912, withdrew fellowship from two members for joining the Morman and Methodist Churches.*
- *1916, delegates to Enon Association were to call for letter of dismission from that Association.*
- *1917, elected delegates to the Mountain Association. The pastor resigned and another was called.*
- *1921, motion to ask the Baptist Board for $150.00 for pastoral support. A committee of six girls was appointed to collect money for the financial condition of the church. Clerk called the roll at Conference. Fellowship was withdrawn from one member for heresy (beliefs opposed to the doctrine of a church or denying the faith).*
- *1925, charges brought against one member for fornication and received her acknowledgement and restored her back into fellowship.*
- *1926, charges against a member for drinking and using profane language.*
- *1944, church agreed to send extra money in the Sunday School treasury to the Orphans' Home.*

The following rules were passed addressing whiskey:

- *March, 1890, resolved that we, the members of Chattahoochee Church will not tolerate the making of spirituous liquor by church members anymore.*
- *3rd Sabbath in April, 1896, passed the following resolution: Resolved that we will not allow any member of Chattahoochee Church to engage in making or selling spirits or malted liquors in any way.*
- *April, 1896, amended resolution concerning making whiskey: Resolved that we will not allow anyone of our members to make, sell, or drink whiskey without it being for medical purposes.*

During the early years of churches, discipline was very strict, and they did not hesitate to bring charges against any member when the membership felt that it was justified. Today, most churches no longer accuse members publicly. Each individual is more responsible and answerable to God, than they are to the individuals holding leadership positions of the church. This is not to say, however, that if a member is publicly living in a way that is unbecoming of a Christian, the member will not be approached by the church leaders in private concerning such actions.

County Line Baptist Church

Cleveland, GA

CONSTITUTED: 1934

PASTORED: Fourteen years, 1945 - 1959

In the mid-1930's, a group of twenty men and women met to form a new church for themselves, their families, and their community. The church was organized as Franklin Baptist Church and met at several locations during the early years of the church. On April 16, 1944, a building committee was organized to begin plans to construct the present structure. It is thought that after the purchase of the property, where the present church building stands, that the name was changed to County Line Baptist Church, because it is so near the White/Hall County boundary line.

Over the years, the church has grown from its original twenty members to nearly 200 today. Many improvements have been made to the building, as it continues to be an important part of the County Line Community.

Claude was the first pastor of the church after the new building was completed. During the years that he pastored the church, the County Line Community was a very close and supportive community, and is still such today. They shared and helped each other in both work, play, and worship. Like other small communities in the area, they were truly neighbors to each other.

Edna and Claude Hood
1950's

Crescent Hill Baptist Church

Route 1
Sautee, GA

CONSTITUTED: 1921

PASTORED: Four years, 1936 - 1940 (approximately)

This beautiful, ornate church is a much-photographed, painted, and admired structure located in the Nacoochee Valley. Captain J. H. Nichols, of Milledgeville, Georgia, had the church constructed along with a beautiful house and other structures which he named West End. Nichols allowed the Nacoochee Presbyterian Church to use the building as their place of worship for several years. Across the road from West End, is the Indian Mound, which has stood guard over the valley for centuries. Atop the mound is a beautiful summerhouse also built under the careful direction of Captain Nichols. All of these structures are of Mid-Victorian design.

In 1893, Nichols sold the property to Calvin W. Hunnicut of Atlanta. In November, 1903, West End was bought by Dr. L. G. Hardman (later to become Governor of Georgia). He renamed the home "Elizabeth on the Chattahoochee," in memory of his mother. It became the Governor's summer mansion during his term in office. Because the Nacoochee Presbyterian Church was no longer holding its services in the nearby church, Dr. Hardman generously presented the unique, little church to a group of Baptists for use as their place of worship. Thirty members decided upon the name of Crescent Hill for their church. Today's membership is approximately 150. The church has also belonged to the White County Baptist Association.

Crescent Hill Church is reproduced on the back cover of this book.

Duke's Creek Baptist Church

Cleveland, GA

CONSTITUTED: 1932

PASTORED: Two years, late 1930's

One trademark for which Claude Hood has always been known, is his good sense of humor. He has always enjoyed teasing and joking. In the days before radio, television, and all the other entertainment forms of today, folks entertained themselves. During his younger days, Claude was certainly never one to pass up an opportunity to play a practical joke on a fellow preacher. In the '30's, and '40's, the visiting preacher, along with Claude, would stay with different members of the church during the week-long, summer revival. Claude tells of sometimes sharing a room with the children for the night, but usually the preachers had a room to themselves.

Rev. Clifford Palmer, a very dear friend and the recipient of many of Claude's practical jokes, helped with services during a summer revival at Duke's Creek. One morning, Claude awoke before Clifford, who seemed to be sleeping very soundly. Clifford's clothes were laying on a chair near the fireplace. Claude just couldn't pass up a golden opportunity to be up to mischief, so, he took Clifford's socks and placed one sock in his coat pocket. Now, what to do with the other sock? It seemed that there was a sizable hole that had been burned beside the hearth. Claude felt around the hole, found a splinter, and hung the second sock on it. Houses during these years did not have sub-flooring, and the hole in the floor allowed the viewer to look directly at the ground under the house.

Rev. Clifford Palmer (left) and Claude, 1930's. The two preachers worked together during the early years of Claude's ministry.

Claude then called Clifford to get up and get dressed for breakfast. Clifford started dressing, but when he got ready to put on his socks, they seemed to have disappeared. He was sure he had placed them on the chair before going to bed. He looked under, over, and between everything in the room — no socks. Claude had stood it just about as long as he could! He tried not to appear to be laughing at Clifford, but Clifford knew him too well. "You took 'em, didn't you? Where'd you put my socks?" he demanded, as he came toward Claude. He was caught. Claude had to retrieve the socks, knowing that the next joke would probably be played on him.

Mt. View Baptist Church

Route 3
Cleveland, GA

CONSTITUTED: 1929

PASTORED: Twenty-nine years, 1932 - 1961

Mt. View Baptist Church was founded on September 7, 1929. The people in this community were meeting in a small frame building known as Hood's Chapel, which was established as an interdenominational church. In the early 1900's, interdenominational to the people of White County, Georgia, meant that the membership would be made up of a majority of Baptist and Methodist. Ed Hood, grandfather of Claude, had deeded the property for Hood's Chapel to "all who will come and worship here." Originally, the chapel had also served as the community school house where Claude's dad attended school. It was not a large building, it had two doors, one on each side, and a chimney for the wood stove. There were no windows, and lanterns or lamps were used for light. The church was usually filled to capacity at worship services. Preacher Jim Nix was one of the last pastors at the chapel.

By 1929, there was a desire to have a nicer and larger building in which to worship, also the Baptist members wanted to establish a Baptist church in their community. The heirs of Rev. E. B. Hunt deeded an acre of land to the community for the purpose of building a church. The tract of land adjoined a family burial plot, in which Rev. Hunt was buried in 1909. During his lifetime, Rev. Hunt had hoped that a church would be built near his home; but, he did not live to see it come to pass.

The charter members were made up of people from adjacent congregations, as well as those from Hood's Chapel, all coming together to form Mt. View Baptist Church. The church, built on a knoll, overlooked the Hunt family burial plot, which became the cemetery of the new church. For this reason, the church was given the name of Mount View, and later it was shortened to Mt. View. Standing on the church property, one also has a wonderful view of the beautiful, rolling hills that gently stretch through White County, in their varying shades of deep blues and greens.

In 1931, Rev. Homer Thomas was called as co-pastor of Mt. View, along with Rev. Hubert Turner. During this time, joint pastors were not uncommon in the area. Claude Hood was elected as assistant church clerk in that same year. In the summer of 1932, during the revival, Claude announced his calling into the ministry, and after assisting in revivals throughout the summer, he was licensed to preach by Mt. View in September, 1932. Baptist ministers were usually licensed to preach for a period of time before they were ordained. That same Conference saw Rev. Thomas and Rev. Turner re-elected as the co-pastors of the church for the coming year.

At the October Conference, Rev. Thomas resigned, stating to the church that it was his belief that when a church had good material available, they should use it (meaning Claude). The minutes show that on November 12, 1932, a move and second were made "to elect another preacher to serve in the place caused by the resignation of Rev. Homer Thomas." A move and second were made and a vote taken "to elect Brother Claude Hood as pastor." Claude had already been called in September as pastor of Tesnatee Baptist Church. Both churches scheduled their services for Saturday before the second Sunday (Conference) and the second Sunday (worship service). The scheduled times were, Conference on Saturday morning at Mt. View, and Saturday afternoon at Tesnatee. Claude was always asked to spend Saturday night in a member's home in the Tesnatee Community. He walked to all of his churches for more than two years. Often, as he passed the houses, the children would come out and walk part of the way with him. It was about five or six miles through the woods from his home to Tesnatee. In good weather, or in bad, Claude would be at church at the expected time. Sunday morning service at Tesnatee was at 11 a.m. Then, it was back to Mt. View for Sunday afternoon service at 3 p.m. Sometimes on Saturday and Sunday he would not have time to eat lunch so he might eat a biscuit on the way.

A minister was not supposed to administer the Ordinances of Christ, conduct Conference, or marry anyone until he had been ordained to preach. Having proven himself worthy to preach the gospel of God and lead the people as God's chosen, a church would form a Presbytery to ordain the minister. Accordingly, after being licensed for a year, on March 11, 1933, during Conference at Mt. View, a motion was carried to set apart Brother Claude Hood to be ordained at the next Conference (the ordination usually took place on a Sunday afternoon, and Conference was left open, until the ordination, after which it would be closed). The following churches were invited: Tesnatee, Town Creek, Philippi, Shoal Creek, Cleveland, and Center Grove.

On April 8, 1933, Brother Claude Hood was ordained at Mt. View Baptist Church. The following information was taken from the minutes of the church and was the standard procedure at that time for the ordination of a minister. Everything was handwritten, so some of the records have faded since being written, and some of the handwriting and spelling were not always easy to read. Thus, should an error be found, it is unintentional.

Georgia, White County April 8, 1933

We the undersigned met by request of Mt. View Baptist church for the purpose to ordain Brother Claude Hood to the work of the ministry. In forming the Presbytery, appointed Rev. W. N. Turner, Moderator, Damascus Church; and Rev. A. R. Ray, Philippi Church, Clerk; Rev. W. Y. Grindle, Mt. Sinai Church; Rev. R. B. Etris, and Rev. H. S. Turner, Town Creek Church; Rev. Homer Thomas, and Rev. S. L. Rogers, Wahoo Church.

Deacons of the various churches: W. Y. Anderson and J. N. Staton, Mt. Zion Church No. 2; J. L. Wright, Friendship Church; H. M. Truelove, Dewberry Church No. 2; J. A. Sutton, Tesnatee Church; Virgil Hunt, J. G. Thomas, and Roy Warwick, Mt. View Church.

To present the candidate to the Presbytery, Brother Boyd Hunt.

To examine the candidate on morals, Rev. R. B. Etris. Spokesman for the candidate, J. G. Thomas. To examine the candidate on faith, Rev. Homer Thomas. After examining the candidate on morals and faith, found him orthordox in faith. Rev. S. L. Rogers to pray the consecrated prayer. Rev. W. Y. Grindle to give the charge to the candidate. To give the charge to the Church, Rev. H. S. Turner. To deliver Brother Claude Hood back to the Church, Brother W. J. Anderson. By motion agreed to dissolve the Presbytery. Rev. W. N. Turner, Moderator; Rev. R. A. Ray, Clerk

The final ordination paper read as follows:

STATE OF GEORGIA - WHITE COUNTY

ORDINATION

This is to certify that BROTHER CLAUDE E. HOOD was ordained to the work of the Gospel Ministry by Prayer and the Laying on of the Hands of the Eldership, on the 8th of April, 1933. He was called to Ordination by the Mt. View Baptist Church, of which he was a member, which had ample opportunity to become acquainted with his piety and ministerial gift.

The Ordaining Council was composed of the following Ministers: W. N. Turner, Damascus Church; W. Y. Grindle, Mt. Sinai Church; A. R. Ray, Philippi Church; R. B. Etris and H. S. Turner, Town Creek Church; Homer Thomas and S. L. Rogers, Wahoo Church. Deacons: W. J. Anderson and J. N. Staton, Mt. Zion Church No. 2; J. L. Wright, Friendship Church; H. M. Truelove, Dewberry Church No. 2; J. A. Sutton, Tesnatee Church; and Virgil Hunt, J. C. Thomas, and Roy Warwick, Mt. View Church; who after thorough examination of the candidate, cordially recommend him for Ordination.

Our Beloved Brother, the bearer of this paper, has therefore the entire approbation of the Ordaining Council on being publicly set apart to preach the gospel and administer the Ordinances of Christ. May he, like Barnabas, be full of the Holy Spirit and of faith, and through him, may many people be added to the Lord.

Rev. W. N. Turner, Moderator
Rev. A. R. Ray, Clerk

During the mid-1950's, the members of Mt. View voted to call Claude Hood as their pastor on an indefinite basis. This meant that the church did not open the floor for the election of a pastor during Conference again, unless, and until he resigned, or the Church membership asked him to resign.

In 1957, construction was begun on a new church. It was built from timber cut on the church's property, and on the same site as the existing structure. A building fund was started, but money still had to be borrowed to construct the new building. Claude was one of five members who signed the loan to borrow the needed money, using his house and property on Mossy Creek as collateral to secure the loan. Additionally, to help cut costs, he and other members of the church dug the foundation for the new church using picks and shovels. In 1958, the cornerstone was laid, dedicating the new brick structure. This building is still being used, however, many improvements have been made over the years to meet the needs of a growing membership. Mt. View has belonged to the White County Baptist Association.

During their twenty-nine years at Mt. View, Claude and Edna worked in all areas of the church. As in other churches, Edna was especially interested in providing an opportunity for the children and young people of the church and community to learn, play, and grow in a happy Christian environment. She served as director, and in other roles, of the Vacation Bible Schools, Sunbeams, G.A.'s, R.A.'s, Sunday School, and also directed many Christmas Pageants. In putting together a Christmas program years ago, most everything was handmade, not bought, so a lot of work was involved. Everything from the costumes, to the set, was made by those helping in the event. The "Christmas Plays" always made the season very special! Often the adults, as well as the young people and even little tots, would don costumes, memorize parts, and become involved. The warmth and love of those times made the meaning of Christmas very real. And, depending upon one's age, the arrival of Santa Claus was either an exciting time, or a time of mild, to absolute, gut-wrenching fear of the jolly old man! Fortunately for Santa, the latter emotion was outgrown, allowing him to retain his popularity over the years. In order to make the projects successful, it took more than one or two members of the church. It would often involve the entire community, and that's what made them special.

Under Claude's leadership, Mt. View Baptist Church evolved into a beckoning light in the area. But on September 30, 1961, he announced to the congregation that he felt his work at Mt. View was completed. After a lifetime of being a part of the Mt. View church and community and serving as its pastor for twenty-nine years, he felt that God was leading him to serve as pastor of another church. During his ministry at Mt. View, Claude saw the early members, who had supported and encouraged him, pass away, and their children, and even grandchildren, fill the void. The decision was a very emotional and difficult one to make; but following God's leadership, he resigned and accepted the call of another church. Mt. View will always be Claude's home, however, and today his membership still remains there, as does Edna's. The church continues serving the community having a present membership of 379.

Rev. Dave Fortner, present pastor of Mt. View, and Claude in 1984.

On August 8, 1982, Mt. View and Center Grove joined in honoring Claude with a special tribute celebrating his fifty years of dedicated ministry to people in the five north Georgia counties in which he pastored. A poem written by Claude's son-in-law, Robert, was read that day, which spoke about the man and his fifty years as pastor to so many friends, and to his family as well.

A SPECIAL MAN

SOMETHING VERY SPECIAL HAPPENED 50 YEARS AGO...
THE LORD TOUCHED A SPECIAL MAN AND GAVE HIM SEEDS TO SOW.
THE SEEDS WERE PERFECTLY PLACED TO DO THE MOST GOOD...
WITH OUR BELOVED FRIEND AND TEACHER, CLAUDE EDWARD HOOD.

HE PASTORED FROM WHITE CREEK, TO AMY'S AND DUKE'S CREEK...
FROM BLUE CREEK AND SHOAL CREEK, TO TOWN CREEK.
FROM CENTER GROVE TO PLEASANT GROVE, TO MENTION A FEW...
FROM MT. ZION TO MT. VERNON, AND HOME TO MT. VIEW.

MANY CHURCHES HAVE BEEN BLESSED BY HIS STEADY PACE...
HE'S KNOWN FOR HIS LOVING SMILE AND FRIENDLY FACE.
MARRIAGES, BAPTISMS, AND FUNERALS FILL HIS MINISTRY...
SEEMS HE'S ALWAYS THERE, WITH NEVER-ENDING ENERGY.

FOR 50 CHURCH YEARS, HE'S LIVED WHAT HE'S PREACHED...
STRIVING FOR GOODNESS, WITH PERFECTION NEVER REACHED.
FOR 72 YEARS OF LIFE, HE'S ALWAYS DONE WHAT HE SAID...
LEADING THE WAY, FOR THOSE NEEDING TO BE LED.

HE SHARES OUR GRIEF, LOVE, AND JOY; SLIGHTING NO ONE...
AND GIVES PRAYERS OF COMFORT AND KINDNESS TO EVERYONE.
SO ON THIS DAY OF CELEBRATION, BEST WISHES WE DO SEND...
TO A PASTOR, HUSBAND, FATHER, AND FRIEND.

Irvin Sutton (right), presents a replica of Mt. View Church, which he built in honor of Claude's 50th Anniversary. Rev. Jimmy Palmer looks on.

Rev. Jim Nix. Pastored Hood's Chapel.

Rev. Jim Young pastored Hood's Chapel and later was called to Mt. View Baptist Church on September 7, 1929.

Rev. Homer Thomas pastored Mt. View Church, when Claude announced his call into the ministry. Claude always referred to him as "his father in the work." Rev. Thomas was called to Mt. View on September 12, 1931, and resigned in October, 1932.

Shoal Creek Baptist Church

Route 2
Cleveland, GA

CONSTITUTED: 1835

PASTORED: 1940 - 1941

&

Having been established in 1835, Shoal Creek Baptist Church is one of the oldest churches in White County. As a result of fire, there are no records available prior to 1906. At that time the church had 134 members. Today's membership is approximately 400.

The original church building was a frame structure with a side door called "the women's door." Later this door was used by most everyone to enter or leave the building. Young people who had a new sweetheart and wanted everyone to notice, usually entered the church through the front doors.

If there was a feeling that the preacher was preaching directly at you that particular Sunday you might could have hidden behind one of the several supporting posts which ran the length of both sides of the sanctuary. These posts supported the building's roof. Heat was provided by a potbellied stove which functioned equally well with wood or coal. Wood was most common, as it only had to be cut and brought into the church. Coal, on the other hand, cost money, and money was very rare!

Shoal Creek was fortunate in having several sites to select from for their baptizing. They sometimes used the Chestatee River at the Coppermines, various fish ponds owned by church members, and in later years, a pool constructed in the churchyard for baptizing. Today's two-story, brick church was erected on the same site as the old frame structure, which was torn down when the new building was completed.

A visitor has only to look and listen to see and know of the great love the members have for their church. The evidence is the pride they take in continuous improvements to make the church better, such as, chimes for the steeple, stained-glass windows, carpeting, and a baptistery. A large majority of other rural churches are also building baptisteries.

Shoal Creek is fortunate to have a "graveyard" that tells a little of the history of its ancestors. The oldest gravestone shows the deceased was born July 10, 1790, and died September 22, 1842.

Although Claude pastored Shoal Creek for only one year, the church and the community have been a part of his life for many years. As a young man, he and his friends would walk to the church for revivals and singings. Special friendships were developed during those times which have lasted a lifetime.

Tesnatee Baptist Church

Blairsville Highway, Route 2
Cleveland, GA

CONSTITUTED: 1836 (estimated)

PASTORED: Eight years (pastored twice)
1932 - 1934 and 1936 - 1942

Tesnatee Baptist Church is thought to be one of the oldest churches in White County. Early records were destroyed by fire in 1900, but it is thought that the church was constructed around 1836 or before. The oldest grave marker in the cemetery shows the deceased died in 1830.

Tesnatee, and many other churches, in keeping their early records of membership, had a record book for the male members and one for the female members. The sexes were not mixed. Not only did they keep the records separate, but in the very early days of worship in the rural mountain churches the men sat on one side of the church and the women on the other. Even husbands and wives did not sit together.

The present structure was built in 1929. Tesnatee belonged to the Chestatee Baptist Association in the 1930's, and later to the White County Baptist Association. Today the church has grown to a membership of approximately 120.

Tesnatee was the first church to call Claude as pastor in 1932. That year he co-pastored with Rev. Hubert Turner. Claude has many wonderful memories of the people and good times shared there. One very special memory was made at Tesnatee after Claude was no longer the pastor. Claude and Edna were married at Tesnatee in 1944, by Rev. Garnett Campbell who was then pastor of the church.

The first two years Claude pastored Tesnatee he walked the several miles from his home to the church. He usually walked part of the way through the woods; it was closer that way. He walked during winters and summers, in good weather and bad. When questioned about the cold, he said that to keep warm, he "trotted." "Then, you didn't notice the cold as much," he said. The weather had to be really bad for him not to go to church, because one thing that he never wanted to happen was for his congregation, however small, to make it to church in bad weather and he not be there.

Whether it was winter or summer, mud was always a problem when it rained in the mountains. During the summer months, if the mud was bad, he would carry his shoes to and from church, so they would not be ruined by the mud.

The Center Of Each Community

Claude says that he was never seriously frightened while walking by himself during those early years. Once or twice he came upon someone who did not look too friendly, but he never had a real problem. It has been said that folks developed "night eyes" to help them see how to get around in the dark back then. Flashlights were not available in the early years, so lanterns were used.

Rev. Luther Bowen (left) and Claude, in the late 1930's.

Rev. Garnett Campbell (left) and Claude. Rev. Campbell married Claude and Edna in 1944.

Rev. Hubert Turner co-pastored Mt. View with Rev. Homer Thomas and in 1932, co-pastored Mt. View and Tesnatee Churches with Claude.

Rev. Joe Poole in the 1930's. Rev. Poole assisted Claude in numerous revivals.

Town Creek Baptist Church

Route 1
Dahlonega, GA

CONSTITUTED: Earlier than 1866

PASTORED: Two years, 1943 - 1945

Although Town Creek Baptist Church is in White County, it does have a Dahlonega, Georgia mailing address. Early records were destroyed by fire; but, those records remaining show that there were memberships in the church as early as 1860.

The property to build the church on was deeded by Joseph Etris in 1871. On August 11, 1922, the church membership voted its approval for the church to be used during the week by the Etris School for the children of the community. Their continued use of the church building for a school was dependent upon two conditions: keep the building in good shape; and pay for any damages caused.

The church records further show that the church organized Sabbath School (now Sunday School) and elected superintendents for the school as early as 1883. The original structure was torn down when the present building was completed in 1949. The new church was built just across the road from the original building. The church has been remodeled and has reached a membership of approximately 180 today. Town Creek Baptist Church was named for a creek which runs nearby.

* * * * *

Rev. Ernest Barden (deceased). Rev. Barden assisted Claude in revivals and taught piano at Cleveland Elementary School.

White Creek Baptist Church

Route 1
Cleveland, GA

CONSTITUTED: 1888

PASTORED: Two years, 1959 - 1961

It is thought that the original White Creek Baptist Church was established much earlier than 1888; however, the early church records were lost, so very little is known about its beginnings. A grave marker in the original White Creek graveyard shows the death as being in 1841.

Including the present structure, there have been five different buildings used by the memberships of White Creek Baptist Church, with three on, or near, the present site. The records show that in 1888, a wooden structure was erected which had two front doors, according to the customary design of that time. These two doors led into two aisles on either side of the church, dividing the pews into three sections.

In 1957, the present church was built. The brick structure has two levels; the sanctuary on the upper level, and the educational rooms on the lower level. The present membership of White Creek Baptist Church is approximately 185.

* * * * *

Rev. Sewell Nix and wife Johnnie. Sewell is the son of Rev. Will Nix.

Rev. Joe Fulbright (left), while pastor of the First Baptist Church in Cleveland, GA, with Graham Hood and Tom Hood (right), during the 1950's.

Old Churches That Live Only In Our Memories

Shoal Creek Baptist Church

Mt. View Baptist Church (pictured on front cover)

Holly Springs Baptist Church

Chattahoochee Baptist Church

The River Baptizings

In the earlier years, the Baptist church in each community held a week of "protracted meeting" or a revival meeting. Services were held each morning and evening during the week. Revivals were the highlight of the summer and were attended by folks from all around the community as well as the surrounding communities. It was a great time for worship and rededication as well as visiting with friends and neighbors. Many people accepted Christ as their personal Savior during these revivals. The custom was then to join the church and publicly announce one's conversion. The church voted to accept the new convert "under the watch care" of the church and recommended them as a candidate for baptism. After which, the new member would be invited to stand at the front of the church and be extended the "right hand of church fellowship" by the members who were present. Then they were considered to be a member in good standing of that church and the Baptist denomination.

The Baptist denomination believes in baptism by complete immersion in water which symbolizes the birth, burial and resurrection of Christ. As Christ died, was buried, and rose on the third day to atone for the sins of the human race, immersion symbolizes Christ's gift to man freeing him from his mortal state. Baptism represents the death and burial of self and the acceptance and resurrection to a new life in Christ.

Claude at Mt. Vernon Church baptizing, early 1940's.

Most communities had special places where they baptized. They used rivers, fish ponds, lakes, and creeks which could be dammed to make them deep enough for baptizing. Later some churches built outdoor pools in the church yards, and today most churches are using baptistries located inside the church. With the fading of the river baptizings, a way of life and long-standing tradition will live only in the memories of a few and in recorded stories and pictures.

At the river baptizing, friends and family would gather on the banks of the river as the candidates readied themselves for baptism. Claude always had a brief devotion prior to entering the water. Often he read the scripture found in Saint Mark, Chapter 1, verses 1 - 11, which recounts the baptism of Jesus by John the Baptist. After a prayer, hymns would be sung as the candidates joined hands and followed Claude into the water.

Testing The Waters

Claude (left) and Rev. Clifford Palmer testing the water.

One beautiful old hymn was always sung at each baptizing: SHALL WE GATHER AT THE RIVER? The chorus was sung: *"Yes, we'll gather at the river, the beautiful, the beautiful river, Gather with the saints at the river, That flows from the throne of God."*

In rivers and creeks there was always the possibility of the dirt shifting in the bed of the stream, causing sink holes and other safety hazards while baptizing. Most of the time the preacher used a long stick to test the water and determine the area and depth in which to lead the candidates to be baptized. Preachers have been known to step into water over their heads, due to holes in the riverbed caused by undercurrents.

On the following pages note that most of the pictures show the markers in the water.

Mt. View Church baptizing, late 1930's.

Baptism By Immersion

Mt. View Church baptizing at Hulsey's Mill, 1930's.

To accomplish complete immersion, the person being baptized is laid back in the water, supported and guided by the preacher. Claude always instructed each individual to cross their arms or clasp their hands in front of them. He felt this made the immersion easier. Over the years, he has baptized young and old, large and small. The oldest person baptized was 76 years old. A few people were afraid of water, or just of being baptized, and they panicked as he started to immerse them, making it difficult to raise them back to an upright position.

Greater care had to be taken when baptizing in rivers, streams, and lakes because the clay beds could cause problems with one's footing. In all of his fifty-five years of ministry, Claude never had a serious problem with any candidate that he was baptizing.

Mt. View Baptist Church baptizing.

Confirmation Of Faith

The confirmation was as follows:

Upon the profession of your faith, and in obedience to the command of our Lord and Savior, Jesus Christ, I baptize thee my brother/sister, in the name of the Father, and of the Son, and of the Holy Ghost. Amen.

With his arm extended heavenward, Claude repeated these same words of faith and obedience prior to the immersion of each individual.

Dewberry Church # 1 baptizing in the Chattahoochee River, 1940's.

Blue Creek Church baptizing at Stovall's Mill, 1930's.

The Center Of Each Community

Claude Has Baptized Three Generations Of His Own Family...

...Edna Burke, his wife-to-be years later (second from right), was baptized by Claude while he pastored Amy's Creek Church. She was fourteen when she was baptized in the Chattahoochee River.

...In 1956, Claude baptized his daughter Claudette, age nine, at County Line Church.

Grandson Craig, age nine, was baptized by Claude in the Pleasant Grove Church baptistry in 1976.

Mt. Vernon Baptist Church

1940's

Baptizing

Chattahoochee Church baptizing in the Chattahoochee River.

Mt. View Church baptizing. Rev. Harry Ragan assisting Claude in baptizing his wife Ethel, in 1959.

Baptizing

Mt. View Church baptizing.

Mt. Vernon Church. To keep their skirts from floating up in the water, women would often pin them between their legs, as pictured at left.

Baptizing

Tesnatee Baptist Church Baptizing, 1930's

Dewberry Church #1 group after baptizing, 1940's.

Blue Creek Baptist Church Baptizing

Rev. Cliff Palmer assisting Claude in the late 1930's.

Great Crowds Gathered On The Banks

Holly Springs Church. Thirty-five were baptized following the revival in the summer of 1948.

Mt. Vernon Church baptizing.

B. C. Grant Church group after baptizing in 1956.

Baptizing

Mt. Vernon Church group after baptizing, 1940's.

New Bridge Church baptizing in Lake Lanier, 1967.

Mt. Vernon Church, 1950's.

County Line Church baptizing in outdoor pool, 1956.

Camp Meetings

More than a religious gathering, camp meeting was an annual, social event to which folks came from near and far. Most camp meetings lasted for one week; some continued for two. They usually took place in August after the crops had been "laid by."

"Tents" or cabins at Mossy Creek Camp Ground. Note the slat benches used in the arbor.

Communities were closely-knit with many common interests. One of these interests was worship. Their religious beliefs were very important to them. It took endless hours of hard work on a farm to keep a large family fed, clothed, and housed. Visiting with neighbors was only possible after all the chores had been completed, and this did not happen often in the earlier days. Sometimes, the community would get together to share work and socialize at the same time, but camp meetings provided an opportunity to briefly escape from the ever-present chores. In those days, it was the nearest a family came to a vacation.

Camp meetings started in "Brush Arbors." This was a covering of brush and branches supported by posts with the sides left open. People came from all around by wagon, horseback, and on foot to the camp ground. Families camping for the week might bring a coop of chickens for eggs and food and the family cow for milk. Other necessities were also brought along to provide for the family and the livestock during the week. Some families slept in their wagons, while others slept in make-shift tents or out in the open.

As camping and worshipping in this manner increased in popularity, permanent arbors were soon built, log cabins and rough lumber "tents" were constructed, and camp meeting became something of a homecoming where the people of God came together to rekindle the fires of faith and to renew and strengthen the bonds of friendship. For many years the tents did not have running water, plumbing,

Mossy Creek Arbor, located in White County.

Loudsville Arbor and cabins, located in White County.

or electricity. Water was carried from a nearby spring, or there was a public well near the center of the camp ground. Today, the tents have been upgraded, and some are equipped with many, modern conveniences. Others still have dirt floors covered with straw or shavings. The arbors are well-lit at night, so there is no longer any need for the oil lamps of yesteryear.

White County has four religious camp grounds. Two were established before White County even existed, while the area was still a part of Habersham County. Mossy Creek, located in the southern part of the county, was established by the Methodist Church in 1832, and Loudsville was established the next year in the northern part of the county. At this time, both are still used annually for a week-long camp meeting. While many attending the services today drive to the camp grounds daily, the cabins and tents are still used by the families who own them.

Black people originally attended both Loudsville and Mossy Creek, but in later years, they established their own camp at Rock Springs, which is near Mossy Creek Camp Ground. Rock Springs was also Methodist in origin, although like the others, camp meeting was attended by all denominations. Union Grove Camp Ground was established in 1925, by the North Georgia Conference of the Congregational Holiness Church.

Even with today's, modern improvements, camp meeting still gives those who attend a brief glance back to another time when life moved at a slower pace. Camp meeting allows one however briefly, to slow down, to worship, and to share in a very different way.

Photograph Album

Photography was one of the greatest inventions introduced to North Georgia. With the camera, special people, places and events could be recorded, enjoyed, and passed on to future generations. In earlier times, as today, photographs are memories of the heart.

Pictured (l-r) at Mae Hood Black's wedding are: Claude, Jesse Black (the groom), Mae, Miss Telford, and Mollie and Willie Hood. 1931.

Mollie Hood stands in front of her house during the 1930's. Notice her stylish coat, also the huge piles of firewood behind her.

J. Wiley Hood, early 1900's.

Friends from the Town Creek Community: (front row, l-r) Guy Allen, Fred Hood, Jesse Thomas, and Oscar Warwick; (back row, l-r) Otho Holman, Roy Warwick, Fred Holman, and Loyd Holman.

Photograph Album

Wiley Black worked at Smith's Soda Shop located "On the Square" in Cleveland, Georgia, during the early 1950's.

Pearl Dixon, Edna's maiden aunt, lived with Claude and Edna for several years and helped care for Claudette when they were away for weeks of revivals.

Edna Burke Hood (left) and Johnnie Dixon Arrendale at their seventh grade graduation from Clarkesville Elementary School in 1936.

Pearl Dixon stands in front of Hubert Burke's homeplace. 1940's.

Photograph Album

Dahlonega, GA. Prisoners being taken from jail in Dahlonega to an unknown destination by Tom Sargent, son of Sheriff John Sargent. Circa 1910.

Cleveland, GA. Brothers, (l-r) Bill, Hoke, and Clifford Campbell standing in front of the White County Post Office which was located "On the Square."

Gainesville, GA. The Princeton Hotel in 1912. Erected in 1887 at the corner of North Main and Washington Streets, it was named the Hudson House, later becoming the Princeton Hotel. In 1959 the structure was torn down. The W. F. Woolworth Company store has occupied the site since 1960.

Photograph Album

Claude (left), Britt and Nancy Whitmire during the 1950's.

Ernest Jarrard (left) and Richard Jarrard are pictured with their mother, Alice Corbin Jarrard. They are in the doorway of her first home after she married. The log cabin was located near the foot of Blood Mountain in Lumpkin County. 1930's.

Leonard and Mary Little lived in the Mt. Vernon Community during the 1940's.

With help of friends...J. W. Lancaster (left) and Jewell Barden helped Claude regain his strength and use of his legs by walking with him everyday after he had back surgery in 1963.

Photograph Album

Pictured (l-r) are: Ruby Hunt and Tommy Hunt (deceased), Mr. and Mrs. William Hood, and Claude at the 25th Wedding Anniversary of the Hood's. Claude married them, and the Hunt's were present at the wedding.

Ellis and Audrey Dixon, uncle and aunt of Edna Hood. They also helped Claude and Edna plan their secret wedding in 1944.

Men's Sunday School Class of the First Baptist Church in Cleveland, GA.

The Thomas Family, (front row, l-r) Jimmie Thomas and Dean Thomas (deceased); (back row, l-r) Marie Thomas and Junior Green, Dot and Guy "Speedy" Thomas. Claude stayed overnight in the Thomas' home during the early days of his ministry and graduated with Speedy.

Photograph Album

Sisters, Robie and Maybell Gailey of B. C. Grant Community in Habersham County.

Garvis Chambers and Claude enjoy a good laugh about the "good old days."

Mae and Gordon Savage during a visit with Claude in Cleveland.

Pictured are (l-r): Claude, Colvin and Georgia Ingram, and Edna. Claude graduated from high school with Georgia.

Bibliography

Bachtel, Douglas C. THE GEORGIA COUNTY GUIDE. The Cooperative Extension Service. The University of Georgia College of Agriculture. Athens, Georgia. 1987.

Bagley, Garland C. HISTORY OF FORSYTH COUNTY, GEORGIA. Easley, South Carolina: Southern Historical Press, Inc., 1985.

Bass, Addie. EARLY HISTORY OF HABERSHAM. Tri-County Advertiser, June 16, 1927.

Bayly, Joseph. THE VIEW FROM A HEARSE. Elgin, Illinois: David C. Cook Publishing Company, 1969.

Blanton, H. J. WHEN I WAS A BOY. Columbia, Missouri: E. W. Stephens Publishing Company, 1969.

Bonner, James C. GEORGIA. A STUDENT'S GUIDE TO LOCALIZED HISTORY. New York: The R. L. Bryant Company, 1982.

Brice, W. E. A CITY LAID WASTE. (Gainesville Correspondent The Atlanta Journal and Constitution and Associated Press) Gainesville, Georgia, 1936. Reprinted, Gainesville, Georgia: Georgia Printing Company, 1986.

Cain, Andrew W. THE HISTORY OF LUMPKIN COUNTY, FOR THE FIRST HUNDRED YEARS 1832 - 1932. Spartanburg, South Carolina: Atlanta, Georgia: Stein Printing Company, 1932; Reprinted, 1978.

Caldwell, Erskine. DEEP SOUTH, MEMORY AND OBSERVATION. Athens, Georgia: Brown Thrasher Books. The University of Georgia Press, 1980.

Church, Mary L. THE HILLS OF HABERSHAM. Atlanta, Georgia: Foote and Davies, Inc., 1962.

CORNELIA, GEORGIA. THE FIRST ONE HUNDRED YEARS. The Centennial Committee for Cornelia. The First One Hundred Years, 1987.

Dixon, B. Aldon. THE DIXON-SOSEBEE FAMILY HISTORY. Arkadelphia, Arkansas, 1980.

Douglas, Ann. "Heaven Our Home: Consolation Literature in the Northern United States, 1830-1880." D. E. Stannard (editor), DEATH IN AMERICA. Philadelphia: University of Pennsylvania Press, 1975.

FOXFIRE. Vol. 3, Number 3, Winter, 1969. Rabun Gap, Georgia.

French, S. "The Cemetery as a Cultural Institution: The Establishment of Mount Auburn and the Rural Cemetery Movement." D. E. Stannard (editor), DEATH IN AMERICA. Philadelphia: University of Pennsylvania Press, 1975.

Fuller, Daniel P. GIVE THE WINDS A MIGHTY VOICE, THE STORY OF CHARLES E. FULLER. Waco, Texas: Word Incorporated, 1972.

Genevay, Bonnie. "Loss of a Mother, A Personal Account." GENERATIONS, Spring, 1987.

GEORGIA BAPTIST DIGEST, 1987. Volume XLVII.

Gillespie, Paul F. FOXFIRE 7. Garden City, New York: Anchor Press/Doubleday.

Gore, Michael. 1003 HOUSEHOLD HINTS. New York, New York: Bankers Community Service Company, 1948. (Revised Edition, 1951, by Mark Elliott, Inc., New York, New York).

GRIER'S ALMANAC. Grier's Almanac Publishing Co., Atlanta, Georgia.

Griffis, Julie. TOMBSTONES. Rome, Georgia, March 8, 1987.

Haberstein, Robert W. and Lamers, William M. FUNERAL CUSTOMS THE WORLD OVER. Milwaukee, Wisconsin: Bulfin Press, 1974.

Haberstein, Robert W. and Lamers, William M. THE HISTORY OF AMERICAN FUNERAL DIRECTING. Milwaukee, Wisconsin: National Funeral Directors' Association, 1955, 1962, 1981.

Harshaw, Lou. THE GOLD OF DAHLONEGA. Asheville, North Carolina: Hexagon Company, 1976.

House, Alvin G. NUGGETS OF BAPTIST BELIEF. Nashville, Tennessee: Broadview Press, 1941.

A HISTORY OF WHITE COUNTY, 1857-1980.

Hadler, Thomas W. and Schratter, Howard A. THE ATLAS OF GEORGIA. Athens, Georgia: Institute of Community and Area Development, The University of Georgia, 1986.

Hulsey, Anges. "Skitts Mountain." RURAL GEORGIA. Atlanta, Georgia: IPD Printing and Distribution, Inc., July, 1985.

Kahn, E. J., Jr. FROM RABUN GAP TO TYBEE LIGHT. Atlanta, Georgia: Cherokee Publishing Company, 1978.

Karcher, Charles J. "Higher Education and Religion: Potential Partners in Service to the Rural Elderly." EDUCATIONAL GERONTOLOGY, 1980. Washington, D.C.: Hemisphere Publishing Corporation.

Kollock, John. THE LONG AFTERNOON. Lakemont, Georgia: Cobble House Books, 1978.

Kollock, John. THESE GENTLE HILLS. Lakemont, Georgia: Cobble House Books, 1976.

Lerner, Gerda. A DEATH OF ONE'S OWN. Madison, Wisconsin: The University of Wisconsin Press, 1985 (Simon and Schuster, Inc., 1978).

Lohmann, Nancy. "Aging in the Rural South." SYMPOSIUM ON REGIONAL PERSPECTIVES ON AGING: GROWING OLD IN THE SOUTH. Toronto, Canada, 1981.

Lester, James Adams. A HISTORY OF THE GEORGIA BAPTIST CONVENTION, 1822-1972. Nashville: Curley Printing Company, Inc., 1972.

McRay, Sybil. HISTORY OF THE CHATTAHOOCHEE BAPTIST ASSOCIATION AND ITS AFFILIATED CHURCHES, 1826-1976.

McRay, Sybil. PICTORIAL HISTORY OF HALL COUNTY TO 1950. Dallas, Texas: Taylor Publishing Company, 1985.

McRay, Sybil Wood. THIS 'N THAT. HISTORY OF HALL COUNTY, GEORGIA. 1973.

Bibliography

Martin, Harold. HAROLD MARTIN REMEMBERS A PLACE IN THE MOUNTAINS. Atlanta, Georgia: Peachtree Publishers, Ltd., 1979.

Miller, Zell. THE MOUNTAINS WITHIN ME. Atlanta, Georgia: Cherokee Publishing Company.

Mitchell, Curtis. CAVALCADE OF BROADCASTING. Chicago, Illinois: Follett Publishing Company, 1970.

Porter, Allene L. I REMEMBER..."T" MODEL DAYS. Toccoa, Georgia: Commercial Printing Company, 1984.

"Public Use Samples of Basic Records From the 1970 Census." U. S. Bureau of the Census. Washington, D.C.: U.S. Government Printing Office, 1972.

Purcell, Mr. and Mrs. Claude. THE WHISKEY PREACHER.

Ray, Lisa. AGRICULTURAL HERITAGE OF GEORGIA. Georgia Department of Agriculture, Atlanta, Georgia, 1985, Second Printing.

Rupnow, John and Knox and Ward, Carol. THE GROWING OF AMERICA, 200 YEARS OF U.S. AGRICULTURE. Fort Atkinson, Wisconsin: Johnson Hill Press, Inc., 1975.

Sams, Ferrel. RUN WITH THE HORSEMEN. Atlanta, Georgia: Peachtree Publishers Limited, 1982.

SEARS, ROEBUCK AND COMPANY, INC. CONSUMERS GUIDE. Fall, 1900. Northfield, Illinois: DBI Books, Inc., 1970.

Shadburn, Don L. PIONEER HISTORY OF FORSYTH COUNTY, GEORGIA. Roswell, Georgia: W. N. Wolfe Associates, 1981.

Smith, B. J. and Parvin, D. W., Jr. "Corporative Levels of Rurality." FACULTY SERIES. (No. FS74-2 Agricultural Economics). Athens, Georgia: University of Georgia Press, 1974.

Watkins, Floyd C. and Watkins, Charles Hubert. YESTERDAY IN THE HILLS. Athens, Georgia: The University of Georgia Press, 1973; Brown Thrasher Books, 1982.

Wigginton, Eliot. FOXFIRE 4. Garden City, New York: Anchor Press/Doubleday, 1977.

Wigginton, Eliot. FOXFIRE 9. Garden City, New York: Anchor Press/Doubleday, 1986.

Williams, Rob. GEORGIA 2000. Athens, Georgia: Williams Printing Company, 1986.

ROME NEWS - TRIBUNE, "Originality Shines On Tombstones."

THE ATLANTA JOURNAL AND CONSTITUTION, ATLANTA WEEKLY, "Months of Sundays." Atlanta, Georgia, February 22, 1987. Lee Walburn.

THE ATLANTA JOURNAL AND CONSTITUTION, ATLANTA WEEKLY, "Legends of the Little People." Atlanta, Georgia, October 11, 1987. Ron Martz.

THE ATLANTA JOURNAL AND CONSTITUTION, "The Georgia Mountains, Christmas was like Beacon on Dark Night." Atlanta, Georgia, December 22, 1985. Ruth L. Godbold.

THE ATLANTA JOURNAL AND CONSTITUTION, "East Cobb's Last Holdout." Atlanta, Georgia, July, 13, 1986. Sam Heys.

THE ATLANTA JOURNAL AND CONSTITUTION, ATLANTA WEEKLY, "God's Country." Atlanta, Georgia, February 22, 1987. Randall W. Eidson.

THE DAILY TIMES, "Sesquicentennial Edition." Gainesville, Georgia: Sunday, March 23, 1969.

THE TELEGRAPH, (various articles). Cleveland, Georgia.

THE TIMES, "Mossy Creek Campground Alive and Well After 140 Years." Gainesville, Georgia, August 9, 1974.

THE TIMES, "The Great Tornado." Gainesville, Georgia, April 6, 1987.

THE TIMES, "The Valleys Fight To Save Their Heritage." Gainesville, Georgia, February 8, 1987. LaVenier Mize.

THE WHITE COUNTY NEWS, (Various articles). Cleveland, Georgia.

Special thanks to the following individuals for the giving of their time to be interviewed. Their contributions of personal remembrances of their lives in Northeast Georgia during the earlier part of the century was an invaluable source of information for this book.

LEE ARRENDALE	TOM and MILDRED HOOD	LOUDEAN SEABOLT
PAT BARKER	WILLIAM and AVALEEN HOOD	GLADYS SHOOK
JESSIE and MAE BLACK	HENRY GRADY and RUTH HUNT	FORREST SISK
CLIFFORD and MILDRED CAMPBELL	VIRGIL and HASSIE HUNT	DEAN THOMAS (deceased)
GARVIS and ROZELLE CHAMBERS	COLVIN and GEORGIA INGRAM	GUY "SPEEDY" THOMAS
ELLIS and AUDREY DIXON	KENNETH and NELDA KEENE	LILLIE B. TURNER
JERRY and HARRIETT FAULKNER	PAUL LITTLE	RALPH TURNER
ROBIE and MAYBELLE GAILEY	THOMAS MAUNEY	PAT VILES
PORTER GLOVER (deceased)	JACK NIX	GERALD WADE
FRED and IRENE HOOD	REV. HARRY RAGAN and ETHEL RAGAN	BUCK WARD
JOHN and MYRTICE HOOD	JIM ROGERS	LOGAN WELBORN
LESTER and MARY HOOD	GORDON and MAE SAVAGE	DEAN and FRANCES WHITE

The following individuals contributed to the historical information about the churches which Claude Hood pastored. Additional information and history came from church records

Habersham County Churches

AMY'S CREEK BAPTIST CHURCH: DAISY MILES McCOLLUM

B. C. GRANT BAPTIST CHURCH: ANGIE PRITCHETT, ELOISE SHIRLEY, and written histories.

HABERSHAM BAPTIST CHURCH: ELLIS and AUDREY DIXON, and written histories.

NACOOCHEE BAPTIST CHURCH: White County Library.

Hall County Churches

DEWBERRY BAPTIST CHURCH NO. 1: MARY DeLONG and written histories.

DEWBERRY BAPTIST CHURCH NO. 2: MARY NELL WHITE and written histories.

ENON BAPTIST CHURCH: TERESA JACKSON.

HOLLY SPRINGS BAPTIST CHURCH: PAM OLIVER, FRED and NELLIE SAVAGE.

HOPEWELL BAPTIST CHURCH: written histories.

Bibliography

MT. VERNON BAPTIST CHURCH: FRANCES WHITE, SHIRLEY ALLISON, written histories and "The Times," Gainesville, Georgia.

NEW BRIDGE BAPTIST CHURCH: GURLEY SATTERFIELD written histories, and "The Times," Gainesville, Georgia.

WESTSIDE BAPTIST CHURCH: REV. JAMES YOPP, and written histories.

Lumpkin County Churches

MACEDONIA BAPTIST CHURCH: LOUDEAN SEABOLT and KIM GRIZZLE.

MT. ZION BAPTIST CHURCH: MILTON GRINDLE and JAMES ANDERSON.

Forsyth County Churches

PLEASANT GROVE BAPTIST CHURCH: WILMA WOOD, LYNETTE BENNETT (Deceased) and written histories.

White County Churches

BETHEL BAPTIST CHURCH: written histories.

BLUE CREEK BAPTIST CHURCH: GARVIS CHAMBERS.

CENTER GROVE BAPTIST CHURCH: J. C. ROGERS and written histories.

CHATTAHOOCHEE BAPTIST CHURCH: TELFORD HULSEY, RUTH BARRETT DAVIDSON and written histories.

COUNTY LINE BAPTIST CHURCH: T. LYNN SATTERFIELD.

CRESCENT HILLS BAPTIST CHURCH: BUFORD BAKER and written histories.

DUKE'S CREEK BAPTIST CHURCH: oral accounts.

MT. VIEW BAPTIST CHURCH: ROY THOMAS, FANNIE LOU WARWICK and written histories.

SHOAL CREEK BAPTIST CHURCH: JOHNNY SUTTON.

TESNATEE BAPTIST CHURCH: JEAN N. GILREATH and church records.

TOWN CREEK BAPTIST CHURCH: JANET NIX COX.

WHITE CREEK BAPTIST CHURCH: A. H. PALMER.

Additional historical information from the minutes of the following Associations belonging in the Georgia Baptist Convention:

Chattahoochee Baptist Association, Enon Baptist Association, Habersham Baptist Association, Liberty Baptist Association, White County Baptist Association.

Also, many thanks to those who have provided photographs, other personal and family records, recipes, remedies, sayings, and family stories which have been used in this book. Together, they have given a true reality to the ways of life during: "The Time Was...When Life Was Simple, Faith and Friendship Strong."